APN

3 907

MW00681028

DISCARD

952.045 E61j

Entwistle, Basil.

Japan's decisive decade

Arnett Branch Library
310 Arnett Blvd.
Rochester, N. Y. 14619

Rochester Public Library

SEP   4 1986

SEP   4 1986

JAPAN'S DECISIVE DECADE

JAPAN'S DECISIVE DECADE

How a determined minority
changed the nation's course
in the 1950s

BASIL ENTWISTLE

GROSVENOR BOOKS
LONDON · MELBOURNE · WELLINGTON
BRIDGEPORT, CONN

087

First published 1985 by
GROSVENOR BOOKS,
54 Lyford Road, London, SW18 3JJ

21 Dorcas Street, South Melbourne,
Victoria 3205, Australia

P.O. Box 1834, Wellington,
New Zealand.

540 Barnum Avenue, Bridgeport,
CT 06608, USA

© Basil Entwistle 1985

ISBN HB 0 901269 85 9
ISBN PB 0 901269 86 7

All rights reserved, including the rights
to reproduce this book, or parts thereof,
in any form, without the prior permission
of the publisher.

British Library Cataloguing in Publication Data
Entwistle, Basil
    Japan's decisive decade: how a determined
    minority changed the nation's course in the 1950s.
    1. Japan—History—1945–
    I. Title
    952.04'5   DS889
    ISBN 0–901269–85–9
    ISBN 0–901269–86–7 Pbk

Library of Congress Cataloguing in Publication Data
Pre-assigned Card No. 85/047506

Cover design by W. Cameron-Johnson

Phototypeset by Input Typesetting Ltd., London, SW19
Printed and bound in Great Britain
by William Clowes Ltd., Beccles and London

CONTENTS

CONTENTS

ILLUSTRATIONS

ILLUSTRATIONS

Photography: Arthur Strong, Robert J. Fleming, David Channer and others.

ACKNOWLEDGMENTS

Many people had a part in creating this book. First and foremost were the Japanese whose valiant work I have tried to chronicle.

There were a dozen or more from overseas, in addition to those whose names appear in these pages, who contributed greatly, both in the front lines and behind the scenes. Among them were Len Allen, Stephanie Ashton, Hope Ayer, June Blair, Edward Goulding, Dick and Frances Hadden, Nancy Jarvis, Brenda McMullen, Nellie Mitani, Stuart and Polly Ann Smith, and Tapscott and Frances Steven.

Professor Ezra Vogel helped steer my research.

Some life-long friends encouraged, urged and advised me in the writing – especially Ken Twitchell, Garrett Stearly, John and Denise Wood and Dave Carey.

Kirsten Larsen typed and re-typed.

And Jean, my wife, Vee, our daughter, and Fred, our son, enabled, endured and enjoyed those eventful years in Japan.

To all of them, great gratitude.

B. R. E.

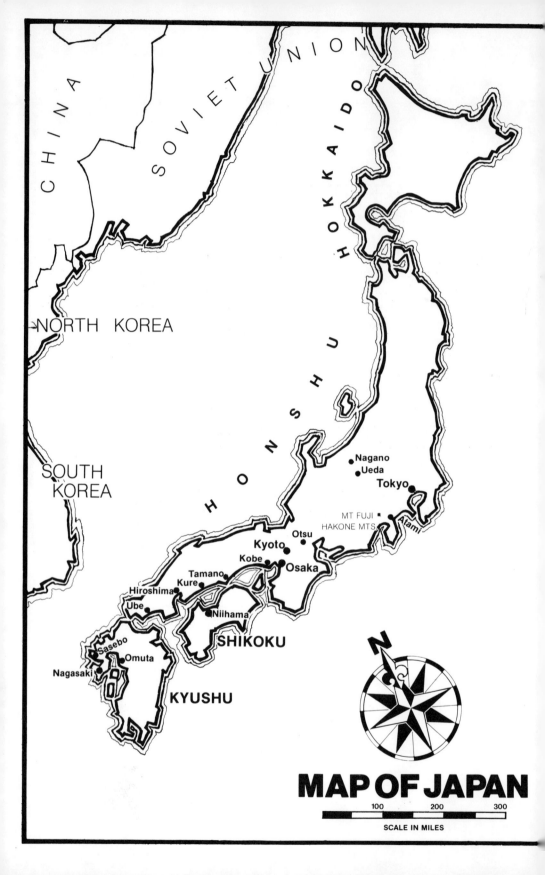

CHINA

SOVIET UNION

HOKKAIDO

NORTH KOREA

HONSHU

SOUTH
KOREA

Nagano
Ueda
Tokyo

MT FUJI
HAKONE MTS.
Atami

Otsu
Kyoto
Kobe
Osaka
Tamano
Kure
Hiroshima
Ube
Niihama

SHIKOKU

Sasebo
Omuta
Nagasaki

KYUSHU

N

MAP OF JAPAN

100   200   300

SCALE IN MILES

JAPANESE NAMES

Author's note: This brief description of men and women who appear frequently in the text may help readers unfamiliar with Japanese names. I have adopted the Western style of placing given names before family names. Use is frequently made of first names or their abbreviation – for example, 'Sumi', for Takasumi Mitsui. This usage was uncharacteristic of Japanese at the time, but reflects their close association described in these pages. I also use the title 'Senator' for Members of the Upper House of the Diet, the House of Councillors. The use of lower case 'c' for conservative is deliberate. There were two conservative parties but neither was known by that name.

Araki, Eikichi	Ambassador to the United States, then Governor of the Bank of Japan.
Hamai, Shinzo	Mayor of Hiroshima.
Hatoyama, Ichiro	Political rival to Prime Minister Yoshida, and his successor as Premier.
Honda, Chikao	President of *Mainichi*, largest newspaper in the 1950's.
Horinouchi, Kensuke	Pre-war Ambassador to the United States; in charge of training post-war diplomatic corps; then Ambassador to Taiwan.
Hoshijima, Niro	Veteran conservative Member of the House of Representatives; Speaker in the late 1950's.
Ichimada, Hisato	Governor of the Bank of Japan; then Minister of Finance under Hatoyama.

Ishikawa, Ichiro	President of the most powerful business organisation, *Keidanren*, (Federation of Economic Organizations).
Ishizaka, Taizo	Acknowledged business leader in the 1950's; President of Toshiba; Chairman of the National Productivity Council.
Kajii, Takeshi	Governor of the government-owned Telecommunications Corporation.
Kataoka, Yoshinobu	A director of the National Railways.
Katayama, Tetsu	Only Socialist Prime Minister.
Kato, Kanju	Veteran Marxist agitator; then Socialist Member of the House of Representatives.
Kato, Shidzue	Wife of Kanju; former Baroness Ishimoto; prominent activist for social reforms; Member of the Upper House (House of Councillors).
Kimura, Kozo	Senior official in the National Rural Police; then chief of security section of the Yoshida Cabinet.
Kishi, Nobusuke	Conservative Prime Minister, 1956–60.
Kitamura, Tokutaro	Banker; conservative Member of the House of Representatives, briefly Minister of Finance.
Kubo, Hitoshi	Chairman, National Telecommunications Workers Union; then Member of the House of Councillors.
Kuriyama, Chojiro	Conservative Member of the House of Representatives.
Mitsui, Takasumi	Brother of the head of the powerful Mitsui family (familiarly known as 'Sumi').
Mitsui, Hideko	His wife; also a member of the Mitsui family.
Nakajima, Katsuji	Injured by the Hiroshima bomb; Executive, All Japan Metal Workers Union.
Sogo, Shinji	Governor of the National Railways.

Sohma, Yasutane	Former viscount; landowner, businessman.
Sohma, Yukika	His wife; leader in women's rights.
Sohma, Toyotane	Brother of Yasutane Sohma (familiarly known as 'Toyo').
Sohma, Tokiko	Wife of Toyo.
Sumitomo, Kichizaemon	Head of the Sumitomo family (familiarly known as 'Kay').
Suzuki, Eiji	Chief of the Osaka Metropolitan Police.
Suzuki, Tsuyoshi	Chairman, Telecommunications Workers Union; then Member of the House of Councillors.
Yamada, Setsuo	Socialist Member, House of Councillors from Hiroshima; National Executive, Government Workers Union.
Yamahana, Hideo	Chairman, Chemical Workers Union; Socialist Member, House of Representatives.
Yanagisawa, Renzo	Chairman, Ishikawajima Shipyard Workers Union; then Chairman, National Shipyard Workers Union.
Yoshida, Shigeru	Conservative Prime Minister of the post-war years.

FOREWORD

In just forty years Japan has risen from the ashes of the Second World War, from a position of weakness to becoming one of the economic powers of the advanced industrial world.

When I think of those days I feel I am living in a different age. The greatest problem of that time was how to feed a hundred million people. It is hard to appreciate now the confusion of ideas which pointed to everything old as wrong. Democracy had been introduced as a standard-bearer of the new age, but without knowledge of its essence we were at a loss how to implement it. To borrow the words of the late Mr Taizo Ishizaka, democracy came into post-war Japan with the force of a high pressure fire hose filling a goldfish bowl, creating great confusion.

It was at that time that Moral Re-Armament helped the political, financial and labour leadership of Japan to realize that a sound society must be based on universal moral standards. As President of Ishikawajima Harima Heavy Industries I had personal experience of a full scale change brought to the company through this influence.

Basil Entwistle spent eight years in Japan under the guidance of Dr Frank Buchman. I am very pleased that the story of his work and experience here is now in print. The book is a valuable contribution to understanding the hidden ideological developments in politics, industrial relations and economic life, as well as the international relations of the post-war period. I commend it particularly to all who are interested in Japan.

Toshiwo Doko
Honorary Chairman, *Keidanren*
Federation of Economic Organizations

PROLOGUE:

DECISIVE DECADE

This is an untold story of post-war Japan. Why tell it now? There has already been a flood of books and articles about the country's 'economic miracle' ever since the world was startled by the ability of the Japanese to produce automobiles, television sets, watches, not only more cheaply, but of bettter quality than those of Western industrial nations.

Much of this writing is perceptive, tracing Japan's economic success to her culture and customs. Increasingly, observers of the Japanese scene seem to be realizing that the most characteristic feature of her recovery is not techniques or methods or material circumstances, but an enlightened view of human relations. It has become apparent that the Japanese worker, at least in the major companies, is highly productive because he is treated as a person, not just as a means of production; he has the security of belonging in a close-knit community which cares for his needs; he is included in decision making; and he feels his contributions are important.

But it would be easy to assume from what has been written that the country's resurgence was an automatic process resulting from traditional ways of living and working. I do not believe this is so. Perhaps no other great nation has been as open to new ideas as was Japan during the years following World War II. Her people were confronted by basic choices and had to reach some fundamental decisions.

Among the most insistent ideas competing for acceptance in the economic area were Marxist class war and Western style industrial confrontation. Japan could well have followed either of these paths. She did not, largely because a third way was demonstrated by some of her citizens. It was a way which combined the best of her traditional culture with a realistic response to the problems of the

1

times. And it proved to be a road, not only to economic recovery, but to a renaissance in many areas of national life.

It was my privilege to come to know and work with many of the post-war giants of the decisive decade of the 1950s. Through the efforts of a remarkable network of leaders in government, politics, finance, industry, the labour movement, education, the best of Japan's heritage was preserved at a time when it was in danger of being rejected, and sound ideas from overseas were accepted among a welter of post-war choices. These men and women practised a philosophy which led Japan away from the failures of the past and through many of the pitfalls of the present. They received sufficient support from ordinary citizens to ensure that the country built securely for the future.

Some of them also pioneered in restoring healthy relations with former enemies, especially those Asian neighbours who had suffered severely at the hands of the Japanese military during World War II. This healing of hurts and hates was essential for commercial as well as diplomatic ties, and came at a moment when overseas markets were crucial for the country's resurgent industries.

I started to set these events down on paper for my grandchildren. Friends persuaded me to write for a wider readership, feeling that the achievements of those who worked together to lead Japan in the right direction were significant for our times. What can we learn from them? It would be foolish to dismiss them as exclusively inherent in Japanese culture; they were also the product of moral and spiritual resources. And it would be equally short-sighted to try to emulate the economic gains without recognizing that they were made at the expense of the environment and the weakening of the country's infrastructure, in such areas as housing, roads, sewerage and social security.

What *is* applicable to today's world is the spirit of those who worked together to lead Japan in the right direction. Without a comparable character change, can we find lasting solutions to the massive problems which face us?

1

EARLY ENCOUNTERS

On a hot June morning in 1948 I stood on a San Pedro dock, watching a small, shabby Mitsui Line freighter emerge from the smog over Los Angeles harbour. I was waiting to welcome a party of nine Japanese, the first group of civilians to be permitted to leave their country after the war, other than some technicians whose services were required by the US military. It had taken prolonged negotiations with General MacArthur's Occupation staff and the intervention of thirty US Congressmen to secure their travel permits.

They were coming to the United States to attend an international conference whose purposes, they felt, were important to Japan at that moment. The country from which they had sailed was a devastated land, her cities in ruins after World War II, and her people close to starvation. Japan was a proud country, defeated for the first time in her history, bewildered by the passing away of the old order – the divinity of the Emperor, the loyalties of a semi-feudal society, the dreams of an Asian empire.

MacArthur's Occupation Forces had maintained order, authored a new democratic constitution and sweeping social reforms, and kept the population alive. But as the day-to-day business of making a living became more secure, people were casting around for new foundations to take the place of those which had been destroyed. Perhaps never in history was a country so open to new ideas and new ways. And new ideas there were aplenty, competing for the Japanese heart and mind – Communism, Marxism, democracy, Christianity, Western industrialism.

These nine travellers believed they had found such an idea which could give Japan the moral and spiritual content to fill the vacuum. The central theme of the conference they were here to attend was that necessary political, social and economic changes in society must start with a change of character and motive in individuals; if men sincerely sought to follow what was right in their lives and work, a force was generated to answer problems, personal and national.

Five of this party who stepped ashore were to have a major part in the growth of this moral and spiritual force in their country. One of them, Kensuke Horinouchi, I had come to know in 1935 when, as a callow young man fresh out of Oxford University, I had arrived in Tokyo on my way to China. Armed with an introduction from the popular columnist George Sokolsky, I presented it at the Foreign Office, where Horinouchi was serving as chief of the American section. Almost immediately a serious, quiet-voiced man in his late forties introduced himself. 'George was a good friend of mine,' he said, 'and I'm glad to meet a friend of his.' Horinouchi took me to lunch at his club and asked me what I was doing in Japan. Led on by his questions, I found myself telling him about my life and convictions. As he expressed interest, I gave him some literature about the work in which I was engaged and went on my way.

Next day I was taken out to dinner by Colonel Crane, American military attaché, and over the *sukiyaki* meal he asked me what I had been doing in Tokyo. 'Good God!' he exclaimed, when I mentioned my visit with Horinouchi, 'I've been trying unsuccessfully to make an appointment with that man for the last couple of weeks.' Diplomatic tension between the two countries was growing to the point where normal liaison between government representatives was becoming difficult.

Two months later in Hankow, I read in the press the dramatic story of the February 26 assassination plot against government leaders and the attempted coup by rebellious army officers in Tokyo. Before they were subdued they killed the Finance Minister and other officials and seized the Diet building and several government offices in an attempt to force a more militant foreign policy. In the reorganization which followed, the Foreign Minister became Prime Minister and Horinouchi was promoted to Vice-Foreign Minister, one of the most difficult and dangerous posts at that moment. His main responsibility was to act as liaison between the Foreign and War Ministries. The military leaders were openly antagonistic towards the government, which they felt was too mild in pursuing Japan's advance on the Asian mainland. Every day Horinouchi faced possible assassination from young army zealots.

But something had happened in his family to strengthen his determination. On my arrival in Hankow I received a letter from him saying he had taken home the literature I had given him and his wife had read it. As a result of her interest he too had studied it and wanted to know more. I sent them the name of an American friend in Tokyo and in due course heard from Horinouchi through this friend that his wife Toshiko had experienced a spiritual renewal and been freed from the daily dread of her husband's death. She now supported him in his work instead of nagging at him to quit. In his turn, he could carry on his delicate negotiations without the drag of fear and resentment at home.

That summer the Horinouchis invited me to stay with them for a couple of weeks in their Tokyo home. At the time I did not appreciate how bold a move it was for him, as Vice-Minister of Foreign Affairs, to have a Westerner as a house guest. Relations between Japan and Britain and the United States were steadily worsening. Japan was still bitter towards the United States for excluding Japanese from immigration. They were angry at the British for their leadership in the League of Nations' condemnation of Japan for taking over Manchuria and aggression in North China. Rightist movements were whipping up public feeling against both countries, which disapproved of Japanese imperialist aims in Asia.

After a while I noticed that I was being followed. When I asked Horinouchi about it, he smiled and said the security police kept an eye on all foreigners, especially those whose business they did not quite understand – but not to worry! On several occasions he invited friends to meet me. Among the guests were members of his staff who had seen in him a new courage and confidence. He was beginning to create a nucleus who worked with him in his struggle for honesty and integrity.

Horinouchi continued to do all he could to keep his country's foreign relations on an even keel, but he was not in charge, nor was the civilian element in the Cabinet. One year later, the explosive forces let loose in North China proved too strong, and Japan was at war. Nevertheless, Kensuke's work was appreciated by his superiors and it was not long before he was asked to undertake the most difficult assignment, the ambassadorship to Washington. Despite heavy pressure from his government, he maintained honest relations in his dealing with United States officials until he could no longer conscientiously follow instructions from Tokyo. In 1940 he asked to be recalled and had to retire from the foreign service and live under close police scrutiny during the war years.

After the war, the Government was faced with the task of rebuilding its diplomatic corps from the ground up in preparation for the time when the nation regained its freedom and could restore relations with other countries. Horinouchi was put in charge of training a new breed of foreign service officers, a responsibility for which he was well fitted.

As the boat came alongside the San Pedro dock, I recognized two others in the delegation arriving for the conference – Takasumi Mitsui and his wife Hideko, whom I had met in Britain soon after my return from Japan in 1937. Takasumi was the brother of Baron Mitsui, head of the Mitsui family and of the country's largest financial and business complex. Sumi and Hideko, who was a cousin and also a Mitsui, had become bored with the social life of the Mitsui clan, where they saw few outsiders. He entered Oxford University as an undergraduate, taking courses in economics, although he was a graduate of Kyoto University, and had written a book on banking. With his wife and young children he rented a pleasant house on the banks of the Isis and spent more time on the golf course than he did at lectures. One of Sumi's tutors was Alan Thornhill, a lecturer and college chaplain in the university. Sumi had been advised to study the New Testament with him as a means of improving his English. In due course Thornhill's insight and patience led Mitsui to a firm faith in God.

Now, in 1948, they were thinner and looked much older, but their spirits were high, despite the tribulations they had been through. On the same day their two Tokyo homes had been burned to the ground by fire bombs from American planes, and from then on they had been living in the *okura*, the concrete storage house of one of their homes. Like many Japanese, by war's end and afterwards they had little to eat but sweet potatoes, and one of their children had died of malnutrition. Because of their foreign

6

connections they had been closely watched by the police but, being members of the powerful Mitsui family, were never arrested.

Another couple in the party, whom I met for the first time, were Yasutane and Yukika Sohma. Yasu had been a viscount, head of a generations-old noble family with feudal estates in central Japan. At the end of the war, along with the rest of the aristocracy, he had been stripped of his title under the new constitution, together with much of his estate. He was of my age, a whimsical, charming bon viveur. His wife Yukika was a brilliant woman, daughter of Yukio Ozaki, 'Father of the Japanese Diet.' While Mayor of Tokyo in 1912 he had presented the United States with the cherry trees whose blossoms became one of Washington's tourist attractions. His bust now stands in the entrance to the Diet building, honouring him as the pioneer of parliamentary democracy, but for most of his life his crusading spirit kept him in hot water. He battled for democratic processes against the military, big business and the entire feudal establishment. Several times he came close to assassination at the hands of reactionaries. On one occasion Yukika fled with him from their home, scaled a wall and hid in a garden. She not only shared his adventures, but flouted tradition at every opportunity, including riding a motor-cycle, unheard of in those days. Her entry into the oppressive atmosphere of the Sohma family had proved a traumatic experience for everyone, until she and her husband found a satisfying basis for their marriage.

The international conference into which the Sohmas and their companions plunged had been called together in Los Angeles by Moral Re-Armament. This movement had been born in the years immediately before World War II out of the conviction of an American, Frank Buchman, that the democracies must meet the threat of Nazi Germany not just with military re-armament, but with a rebirth of moral and spiritual strength. MRA, as it was popularly known, spread rapidly from person to person and continent, and now in Los Angeles the Japanese had the opportunity to meet with men of affairs from the West who were grappling with problems of post-war rehabilitation.

In 1948 the Cold War was at its height. Western Europe was facing Russia's encroachments to the East, dramatized by her blockade of West Berlin. In Asia, North and South Korea were established as rival ideological nations. In this setting, the feelings of the Japanese were well expressed by Kensuke Horinouchi in a talk to the conference:

'The new constitution has given us the machinery of democracy. Even more important is a new spirit which will make it work. In the last year I have seen the whole structure of democracy collapse in country after country. There are in the world forces aimed at its destruction, threatening even countries where forms of democracy have existed for many years. It is absolutely essential in Japan that we have a working answer for these forces from the very start. I am attending this assembly to meet leaders from many countries whose first concern is to create a world-wide force which will give democracy an answering ideology. Many of us in Japan are not only grateful for the material aid we are receiving; we are even more grateful for Moral Re-Armament. It is the moral and spiritual dynamic which can make democracy work.'

After the conference most of the Japanese returned home, but the Sohmas were invited to travel with an international MRA team in Europe. On their way back through the States six months later, they stopped to see my wife Jean and me in Atlanta, where we were busy with a series of meetings. They made a strong plea that I would help them take advantage of the situation in Japan.

'The country is wide open to MRA,' Yukika said, 'and now is the time to reach out to our leaders. We have the openings and people are hungry for just what MRA has to offer.'

'I would love to be over there with you,' I told them, 'but I can't leave Jean now with a two-year-old daughter and another baby on the way.'

'Why don't you bring the family over? We'll find a home for you.'

'In Japan right now, with everything in ruins?'

'Well, maybe not immediately, but let us work on it. Soon things will improve and we'll be ready for you.'

I smiled and murmured some cordial reply and forgot about the idea.

The following May I was in Louisville, Kentucky, Jean's home town, where our son Fred had recently been born, when I received a cable from Frank Buchman, the founder of MRA, asking me to accompany some distinguished Japanese guests from America to

8

Caux, Switzerland, where Moral Re-Armament had opened an international conference centre after the war. I had no desire to leave my wife and new-born son. Yet I felt it laid upon me to fulfil a commitment more pressing than personal wishes. This was one of many occasions when Jean and I had to make difficult decisions to be apart from the children or each other. But these decisions we made together.

The Japanese party with whom I flew from New York to Geneva was headed by Tetsu Katayama, recently Prime Minister, and now Chairman of the Socialist Party. He was accompanied by his wife, a man secretary and two newspapermen from *Mainichi*, the largest daily – Takahashi, an editor, and Fujimoto, assistant foreign editor. Katayama's overseas trip was hitting the headlines in Japan and he had been commissioned by *Asahi*, the great rival paper, to write accounts of his journey. An intense competition developed between him and the two *Mainichi* men to scoop each other during their travels. For the next two and a half months these Japanese were my constant companions as I shepherded them through the Caux conference, in Europe and back across the United States. Katayama had been a college professor, an intellectual reserved to the point of gruffness. His replies to questions and his comments often sounded like grunts, which his secretary translated into voluble, but confusing English. Mrs Katayama was a warm-hearted and motherly soul.

Their arrival at Caux was a startling experience for the Katay-amas. The place itself was spectacular, a large hotel complex capable of accommodating one thousand, perched on a mountain ledge two thousand feet above the Lake of Geneva. Every kind of person and many nationalities flocked there during these post-war years – statesmen, bankers, industrialists, farmers, factory workers, housewives. Konrad Adenauer of West Germany and Robert Schuman of France attended conferences and paid tribute to the spirit of Caux as a major factor in reconciling their two countries and laying the foundations for the economic recovery of Western Europe. While the Katayamas were there a delegation of US Congressmen arrived on an official mission to report to Congress on MRA's role in that recovery.

The Japanese had little understanding of Moral Re-Armament when they arrived, but they began to grasp that its basic aim

9

was the reshaping of national and international life through the remaking of men. At meetings they listened to French and Canadian businessmen who had put care for their employees ahead of profits, German and British coal miners who had turned away from Communism and were greatly increasing productivity, men in public life who were deciding policies on the principle of 'what is right, not who is right.'

The basic need was for a change in the individual, the starting point for sound homes, teamwork in industry and a united nation. MRA was the Sermon on the Mount, expressed in everyday language and modern life. There was no formal membership and the appeal was not just to Christians, but also to men and women of every faith and those who had none.

After a couple of weeks, the Katayama party set off on a tour through the West German Ruhr, Paris, London and across the United States. The delegation was joined by Kensuke Horinouchi, Takasumi and Hideko Mitsui and six young Japanese who had received permission from their government to come for a year's training with MRA. This was the first group of Japanese to visit the Ruhr since the war and their welcome was overwhelming. Both countries had suffered similar experiences of ruined cities, hunger and defeat.

The Lord Mayor of Duesseldorf and a cabinet minister were on hand to meet our plane. Our host, the head of a large copper company, arranged for the group to meet the senior businessmen of the city. In addition to daily luncheons and dinners, there were tours through steel plants, machine works, housing estates and even a coal mine, where the Katayamas, both portly figures, gamely squeezed through steep and narrow tunnels.

The Association of Trade Unions in the British Zone of Germany entertained the party and Hans Boeckler, head of the West German labour unions, welcomed them to his headquarters. Karl Arnold, Minister-President of North Rhine-Westphalia, presided at a banquet given by him and his Cabinet. The mayors of each city entertained them, as did the German Steel Board and the head-quarters of the German Socialist Party. Everywhere the group went there was a sympathetic accord between Germans and Japanese, both defeated people in the recent war. The newspapers clamoured for interviews and covered every event fully.

10

In responding to the welcome of his hosts Katayama had a set speech. He spoke with appreciation of his visit to Caux and paid tribute to 'the two great gifts to mankind from Western Europe, and Germany especially – Marxism and Christian democracy'! Mrs Katayama was not always satisfied with her husband's undemonstrative manner. At a civic reception in the beautiful City Hall of Duisburg she leaped to her feet and said she must add a word. She spoke with great warmth, bursting into tears at one point, and ended, 'I pray that Germany and Japan will make no more political mistakes, but will fight for what is right. The ruined cities of our two countries are the direct result of our mistakes. We women must teach our children the way to a better world.' She received a great ovation.

By contrast, the four days in Paris were quiet, as many were away on their summer vacations. We arrived on the eve of July 14, Bastille Day, the big national holiday, watched a parade marching down the Champs Elysées in the pouring rain, toured Versailles Palace and other sights, and were received at the annual conference of the French Socialist Party. In his speech on that occasion Katayama made a plea for the inclusion of the Japanese Socialist Party in the Socialist International – one of his great concerns. Léon Blum, the veteran head of the Party, greeted Katayama with warmth – which made the day for him.

Then on to London, where a highlight of the week was a luncheon given by Christopher Mayhew, Under-Secretary for Foreign Affairs, at which he included men from Parliament and the Foreign Office who were concerned with Japan. The event was significant because at the time there was still a great deal of anti-Japanese feeling in Britain. Many could not forgive the cruelties inflicted by the Japanese military on their prisoners in Hong Kong, Singapore and Burma. Mayhew asked Horinouchi what he felt MRA could do for Japan. In reply, he said he believed its greatest contribution would be in capturing the imagination of youth, answering Communism, and creating national unity.

The party flew on to New York and ploughed their way through a heavy schedule of events, the most significant being a day spent at the United Nations. Japan had not been admitted to the UN and Katayama and the rest were surprised by the cordiality of the welcome they received from senior officials. Byron Price, Acting

Secretary-General, greeted them in his office. Admiral Nimitz, wartime hero of the battles in the Pacific, and Andrew Cordier, in charge of administration, were especially attentive hosts. The party sat in on a meeting of the Disarmament Commission and heard a typically tough exchange between the American and Russian delegates. Then came a luncheon at the Bankers' Club and a tour of the Stock Exchange arranged by its president.

After sight-seeing in Washington and a busy programme on the West Coast arranged by Japanese communities in Los Angeles, Seattle and San Francisco, the party flew back to Tokyo. Before boarding the plane, the Katayamas expressed their appreciation for all they had received and said they had been given much food for thought. A more immediate positive fall-out from the trip was the flow of articles by Fujimoto, Takahashi and Katayama to their newspapers. As their reports came back to us we found that they had conveyed to millions of readers graphic accounts of the tour and the warm welcome extended to the Japanese. They had also managed to give the public some concept of Moral Re-Armament and its impact on the responsible men and women they had met in Europe and America.

Early in the New Year, 1950, another cable from Frank Buchman launched me again among the Japanese. He asked me and a colleague, Ken Twitchell, to fly as soon as possible to Tokyo to visit some of our Japanese friends about whom he was concerned. Kenaston Twitchell, some years my senior, was the man responsible for introducing me to Moral Re-Armament during my freshman year at Oxford. Ken was now with his wife, Marian, in Princeton, staying with her father, US Senator Alexander Smith. Through the Senator, who was a senior Republican on the Foreign Relations Committee, we were able to expedite our travel documents, which were not easy to obtain, as Japan was strictly controlled by General MacArthur's Occupation Forces. He made an appointment for us with the Under-Secretary of the Army and the latter's word to the Pentagon produced our military permits in record time.

Ken and I landed at Haneda airport in Tokyo on February 3, 1950. As our plane taxied toward the terminal building we saw a military formation drawn up and a band playing. As we watched, General Omar Bradley, American hero of the assault on Hitler's fortress Europe, was given an official send-off by General

MacArthur, Supreme Commander of the Allied Forces occupying Japan, and the man under whose authority we would be operating in the country.

2

WIDE OPEN COUNTRY

Ken Twitchell and I came out of the plane into cold, pouring rain. The terminal building at that time was not the gleaming palace of today, but a cluster of grimy army huts, a dismal scene. We quickly made our way through the formalities and registered at the American Army's civilian visitors desk, where we were allocated a room at the Teito Hotel. The Occupation Forces controlled the essentials of life for all who entered Japan. Foreigners had to stay only in approved hotels; we were not supposed to eat in Japanese restaurants, nor buy articles in Japanese stores.

There was good reason for these regulations. A little more than four years since the surrender, Tokyo had not yet fully recovered from the war. I had been in London during and after the Nazi blitzes and had served in the US Army occupation of West Germany immediately after the war, so scarred cities were familiar to me. But here, although ruins had been cleared away and many houses, offices and factories rebuilt, there were still acres of empty land, testimony to the vast fire bombing by American planes. The stores, we soon found, were pathetically short of consumer goods, including food. And it was obvious that most people were making do with old clothes. Almost the only automobiles on the streets were US Army cars, since no gasoline was available for civilians. The taxis we used were powered by great charcoal furnaces lashed to their rears.

We wondered what manner of reception, as Americans, we would receive. Polite, no doubt, but how sincere? How much would Japanese listen to any ideas of ours? We need not have been concerned. From the start we found an astonishing openness, curiosity and even hunger for any information about the outside world or insight into their own country we might provide. Our first news conference was symbolic of this attitude. After welcoming us, Horinouchi, the Mitsuis and Sohmas took us to meet members of the press awaiting us at the hotel.

The reporters at this and many subsequent interviews had little of the cynicism which we had come to expect from some of their counterparts in the West. Next morning we read in the papers a straightforward account of what we had said. The keynote of my remarks was reported as, 'MRA gives everyone a chance to remake the world – the kind of world we long in our hearts to live in.' *Mainichi* quoted Ken's evaluation of the impact of MRA on West Germany and other parts of the world. We read, somewhat to our surprise, that we 'are expected to meet with General Douglas MacArthur and other Occupation officials as well as Japanese notables' during our stay.

During our flight across the Pacific, Ken and I had tried to clarify the priorities of our mission. Our Japanese friends had told us that they could give us access to influential men and women. Many of these leaders, they said, were concerned with the chaotic impact of new forces on Japanese society: businessmen were being pushed to sacrifice principles for profit; youth were interpreting democracy to mean licence to think or do anything; teachers were having to use new text books written by Marxists; labour unions were mushrooming, with extremists as almost the only experienced organizers; politicians were caught in a race for votes, without clear policies. Our need, therefore, was to present to the leaders in all walks of life attractive alternatives to the ideas they did not relish.

We also recognized that we were entering a country where there was one potent authority – the military Occupation, still in effect the governing force of Japan. Our freedom to operate was depen-dent on the co-operation of the American authorities, who kept a watchful eye on all foreigners.

So on the morning after our arrival we paid our respects to Colonel Larry Bunker, the personal aide to General MacArthur, upon whose sanction everything in Japan depended. Bunker received us cordially and we sketched for him our mission and offered to keep him informed about what we were doing and whom we were meeting. He asked us to contact Colonel Nugent, head of the Civilian Information-Education Section of the Headquarters,

In 1950, the largest delegation to leave Japan since the war arrives in Geneva Airport.

Top: Kensuke Horinouchi, former
Ambassador to Washington (centre)
welcomes the author (right) and Kenaston Twitchell to Tokyo
January 1950

Centre: Taizo Ishizaka, President of
Toshiba (right) and Antonio Banti,
General Director of the Italian
Electrical Industries (left) share the
platform with Frank Buchman at the
1950 summer conference at Caux,
Switzerland.

Bottom: Former Prime Minister Tetsu
Katayama amd Mrs Katayama,
accompanied by Mrs Hideko Mitsui
(left), tour the Ruhr area of West
Germany, 1949.

and report on our activities to him. Nugent, a genial man, said he would look forward to co-operating with us in any way he could.

When we set out with the Mitsuis, Sohmas and Horinouchi to meet their friends we soon found we had underestimated their outreach to the leadership of the country. We also learned that in Japan leadership was more concentrated and interlocking than in most Western nations.

In the course of the next ten days we met with Prime Minister Shigeru Yoshida, the outstanding political figure of the day; the two men who were mischievously referred to as 'the Emperor' and 'the Pope', because of the power they wielded – the Pope was Hisato Ichimada, Governor of the Bank of Japan, which controlled the flow of money in the capital-hungry country, while the Emperor was Chikao Honda, President of *Mainichi*, regarded as the czar of the press world; Yukika Sohma's father, Yukio Ozaki, the veteran parliamentarian; and a number of top businessmen. During those ten days we were also given receptions by the three leading daily newspapers – *Mainichi*, *Asahi* and *Yomiuri* – the Directors of the Bank of Japan, and the Speaker of the Upper House of the Diet.

The receptions by the three newspapers on three successive days were a perfect door-opener to the country, as they reported what we had to say prominently and accurately to some ten million readers. They also invited to the receptions prominent men and women from many fields. The introductions went by so fast that we did not catch all of them. At one reception, for example, a scholarly-looking man remarked towards the end of proceedings, 'MRA seems to be exactly what is needed to save Japan and the world from atomic destruction.' I asked Yukika, who was interpreting for us, who the man was. 'Dr Yoshio Nishina,' she said, 'is our country's leading expert on nuclear energy.'

Prime Minister Yoshida received us in his official residence. A veteran diplomat, he was at home with the Western world. He might have stepped out of the pages of a Dickens novel, with his black coat, pin-striped trousers, stiff white wing collar and pince-nez glasses. He was a gentleman of the old school, conservative in politics, shrewd and courteous. He had worked hand-in-hand with MacArthur to stabilize the turbulent domestic scene in the years after the surrender. Firmly anti-Communist at a time when the extreme Left was gaining a hold on the labour unions, he had the confidence of both big business and of his American overlords. Our conversation on this occasion was chiefly limited to answering his questions about MRA and the purpose of our visit. While cordial in manner, he maintained a sceptical view of human nature and any attempts to better it.

Ichimada, Governor of the Bank of Japan, was bright-eyed, sharp-chinned, with quick, nervous movements and a surprising, high-pitched voice. Like many of his colleagues, he understood English, but preferred to talk in Japanese. Yukika Sohma accompanied us on this and most other visits and was a brilliant interpreter. Ichimada's great concern was to reunite Japan with the rest of the world. On this first of many talks with him he emphasized his belief that the Japanese must accept Moral Re-Armament and apply its moral absolutes to public and private life in order to regain the respect of other countries. He arranged a reception for us to meet his colleagues in the banking world.

Chikao Honda was a brisk, irreverent, high-powered executive, who ruled the *Mainichi* empire and set the pace in the newspaper world. He thanked us for the care we had given his two men on their trip with Katayama and offered the services of his paper to help make our message known to the public. He said he thought Japan needed MRA, but added with a grin, 'I am much too much of a rascal ever to be reformed!' He summoned his editorial staff for a lengthy session with us and urged us to visit Osaka, where *Mainichi* had its headquarters, and nearby Kyoto, the cultural capital of Japan. The Osaka area, known as the Kansai, he assured us, was the mainspring of the country's business and industrial action, and he wanted *Mainichi* to be our host when we visited the Kansai.

Ken and I invited Yukika and her elderly father for lunch at our hotel. Despite his many years, Yukio Ozaki's mind was alert and active. As we left the table he embarked on a favourite theme, the uselessness of the Japanese written language, with its thousands of characters. It imposed an unnecessary burden on children, who also had to learn Western script. As we walked into the lobby, Ozaki, who spoke in the ringing tones of the very deaf, pursued his subject. 'MacArthur missed a great opportunity to abolish the characters. A big mistake. Very shortsighted of him.' The hotel manager hurried up to us and begged Yukika to quieten her father.

Such blunt criticism of the Supreme Commander in a public place was unheard of in 1950.

We were guests of the Tokyo Rotary Club, at that time the largest and most powerful branch in the world, considering the calibre of its members. At two successive lunches we met the presidents of many of the largest businesses. Almost all these men had been elevated to the top positions in their companies at the end of the war, when the senior officers of the basic industries and businesses were purged by order of the Occupation authorities as they were judged to have been deeply involved in Japan's military and nationalistic policies. This new crop of presidents were for the most part middle-aged men who had occupied positions just below the top echelon. They would direct the astonishing 'economic miracle' of Japan's recovery and expansion.

I did not grasp until much later that Ken and I, through the Mitsuis and Sohmas, had been impelled into a unique power group right at the start of our visit. A good deal would be written later about the process of consensus by which the leadership of Japan operated. Yoshida and his political colleagues, Ichimada and his group of bankers, and a circle of top businessmen met in clubs and small associations to confer and shape economic and political policies. Much of their vital discussion and decision-making was done in exclusive restaurants and geisha houses. Over dinner, bankers conferred among themselves and with corporation presidents about, for example, the priority needs for capital expansion in shipbuilding, textiles or chemicals. The appropriate cabinet ministers and government bureaucrats were consulted and advised about budget appropriations and legislation. And out of the give-and-take between these elements emerged the compromises which guided the economic development of the country. Although there was often fierce competition between rival companies, it was a process far removed from the strident free market of the Western democracies and was often the despair of the Occupation, which was dedicated to abolishing cartels, monopolies and price fixing. But it worked with stunning success, as the United States discovered to its dismay some twenty years later.

Ken and I were struck by the hunger of these men for first-hand information about the world – few of them had been permitted to travel abroad. They appeared to welcome new ideas and take

19

what we said seriously. We realized that in this occupied country Americans were treated with exaggerated courtesy, but the hospitality we received went beyond that, and it seemed to us we were treated as VIP's because we represented something they regarded as a vital force in the world and of benefit to Japan.

During these early days we encountered a very different element in society – college youth. We were invited to meet Kisaburo Yokota, Dean of the Law School of Tokyo University, the top institution of higher learning. Its graduates were ensured secure jobs in government, big business or the professions, and competition for entrance was fierce. Ken and I were impressed with Dr Yokota's broad perspective and his concern for the future of his students. An eminent lawyer, he was to become Chief Justice of the Supreme Court. He said that his present generation of students was disoriented by the violent changes the country had suffered. They were uprooted and did not know what to believe.

While we were talking in his study overlooking the central campus plaza, a procession of young men streamed past the windows shouting, singing and bearing large red banners. They were protesting about 'repressive and Fascist regulations' against free speech, academic freedom, and the like. 'Is this a Communist demonstration?' I asked. 'We've read in the papers that they are banned.' Yokota smiled, 'Oh, yes, they are forbidden, but there is a long tradition of campus immunity from the police. They dare not enter our gates, and this poses some problems, because professional agitators can find sanctuary here, even though they have committed crimes.'

The Dean arranged an informal meeting a few evenings later with a group of his outstanding young men, the first of a number of such gatherings. Several had been naval cadets in training at the end of the war and when we talked about moral standards one of them stopped us.

'Are you telling us that absolute moral standards and democracy can go together?' he asked.

'Sure. In fact, democracy will never really work unless it has a strong moral backbone. Otherwise, laws, civic responsibility and the whole social structure collapse.'

'But we understood that moral standards were discredited, along with worship of the Emperor and a belief in Japan's divine destiny.'

Another added, 'In the Navy we were trained to live a very strict moral code. At the end of each day we had to examine ourselves and see any places where we had not lived up to it. You are the first people since the war who've said moral absolutes were right. This is great!'

They had formed an anti-Communist association to try to stem Communist influence on campus, and at first wanted us to endorse and support them. Then they began to see a better way – not bull-headed opposition, but a personal commitment, starting with changes in their own lives, to fight for the moral climate in which the injustices on which Communism thrived could be solved. Some of these young men became our good friends.

Ken and I experienced a totally different side of Japanese life when we spent a weekend in the countryside in mid-February. We were given an official invitation by the city fathers of Ueda, which lay in the mountainous prefecture of Nagano, 120 miles north-west of Tokyo. The largely farming population was one of the poorest in the country and Nagano had the reputation of being a cradle of revolutionary movements. There were known to be Communist militiamen preparing for armed conflict hidden away among the remote villages of this alpine territory.

The city of Ueda looked far from revolutionary as our train rolled into the station on a darkening wintry afternoon. Snow covered the roof-tops and an icy wind blew through the station, where representatives of our sponsoring group stood bowing beside the track. We were driven to a beautiful inn, with kimonoed servants, polished wooden floors, *tatami* mats, communal baths. The staff was lined up in the entrance, bowing, as we removed our shoes in the porch and were escorted to our austere room – the only furniture a low table, the bedding tucked away behind sliding doors. The manager told us that our bath awaited us, but we explained that we were due shortly at an early dinner with the Mayor, and would bathe on our return.

The Mayor, City Council, Chamber of Commerce officials and other senior men were awaiting us in the banquet room of a restaurant. As we entered they sank to their hands and knees and bowed so low that their heads almost touched the floor. We did the same. As we raised our heads, they bowed again. So did we. It was a contest to see who could appear the most humble! They

21

won. Flowery speeches of welcome extolled our virtues and their total unworthiness to be our hosts. I nudged Ken; it was his turn to make a formal reply, saying that the honour was entirely on our side. This custom was already becoming familiar. During our five months in Japan we were given some fifty such formal luncheons and dinners and became adept at graceful but brief speeches before we sat down to eat.

When we returned to our inn the staff was again waiting for us at the front door. There was no central heating, but a charcoal fire burned in the *kotatsu*, a large square hole in the middle of the floor. Our bedding, supported by a wire cage, was rolled out over the *kotatsu* to keep us warm in the freezing temperature. We removed our clothes, donned padded robes provided by the inn and were led along corridors to the bath, nervously wondering whom we would encounter there. A large, steaming bath, junior swimming pool size, awaited us with no one in sight. Our Japanese friends had briefed us on the proper procedure – do your washing in a wooden bucket before entering the bath. Ken was first at the bath and gave a loud exclamation as he dipped a toe into scalding water. We ran in cold water from a large faucet and managed to lower ourselves into just bearable water. Next morning, when we told Sumi and Yukika about our experience, we learned we had made two horrible blunders. First, all the guests had been told by the manager they could not have their baths until the Americans had finished, so they had to wait all evening for their turn. Second, when they did get to the bath, they found the water had been turned 'tepid' by those uncouth foreigners.

After two days filled with meetings and conferences, we spoke at a public meeting which jammed the largest room in the City Hall. After we had spoken we invited questions, and an intense young man at the back of the hall asked, if MRA stood for a change in human nature, why did we not concern ourselves with America, which in his view needed change in a big way? I answered his questions frankly, saying that certainly America needed change as much as any country and there were many Americans committed to that change, beginning with themselves. But a new moral climate in one country was not enough. Japan, which had suffered so much in recent years, could have a great part in helping us proud

Americans to see the need of change. Afterwards the young man came up to talk with us.

His name was Katsuji Nakajima. He had been in Hiroshima when the atom bomb fell and was close to death for several months. His health was still affected by exposure to the nuclear fall out. While he was ill he had received word of the death of his father through malnutrition. His mounting bitterness was fed by Communist friends who convinced him that the bosses and the capitalist countries were responsible for the world's problems. Now married and with young children, he was by talent an artist, but circumstances had forced him to work as a machinist. When we met him, Nakajima was an executive of the All Japan Metal Workers Union, which was dominated by the far Left. Intrigued by what he had heard of MRA and by his first encounter with Americans, he lost some of his hostility as we talked, and when we parted promised to call on us during his next visit to Tokyo.

Next morning in Tokyo we received a visit from another Japanese who had cause for strong feelings towards America. Shinzo Hamai, Mayor of Hiroshima, was brought to see us by Setsuo Yamada, who represented Hiroshima in the House of Councillors and had been our guest in Washington. The Mayor, a tall young-looking man with a ready smile, said he was beset by many problems in his task of rehabilitating the city in which more than 100,000 citizens had been killed by the bomb. He had heard from Yamada about Moral Re-Armament, felt it was a message which his people needed and to which they would respond, and asked Ken and me if we would visit Hiroshima. Yamada reinforced the invitation, saying that the Governor of the prefecture and Hiroshima's leading citizens were waiting for us. The visit was arranged for a month's time.

Yamada then took us to a luncheon he had arranged to meet the Deputy Speaker of the Upper House, the Vice-Minister of Labour and the heads of ten of the more moderate national labour unions with a combined membership of 3,500,000. All that week we continued our round of visits with some of the most dynamic and varied leadership of the country.

Ken and I spent most of a day at the Tokyo Shibaura Company (Toshiba), starting with a tour of the main plant and ending with dinner with the senior officers and an evening of discussion. It

23

Arnett Branch Library
310 Arnett Blvd.
Rochester, N. Y. 14619

was our introduction into the heart of an industrial concern. The company employed more than 20,000 in the manufacture of all kinds of heavy electrical equipment. Because it was strategic in the development of other basic industries it became a prime target for Communist action in the late 1940's. Party members gained control of the newly-formed union after the war and for three years their tactics of slow-downs, sit-downs and strikes, coupled with violence, disrupted operations and almost reduced the company to bankruptcy. Finally the Occupation Forces intervened, along with the government, and Toshiba was able to force the union to oust the Communists from leadership. But at the time of our visit we were told there was still a great deal of friction between the workers and management. The same was true, we were told, in other basic industries, where policies of disruption by Marxist-controlled unions and of repression by management were a far cry from the practice of consensus.

Taizo Ishizaka, installed as President of Toshiba at the height of the violence, had taken a firm line with the union militants and under his forceful management Toshiba had begun to prosper. Before coming to Toshiba he had been one of the most able insurance men, and his main office, facing the Imperial Palace, had been requisitioned by General MacArthur as his headquarters. He was a thoughtful host that evening. He and his directors asked searching questions about our work and seemed especially interested in what we could tell them about creating teamwork in industry.

At the end of that week we received a visit from a representative of a committee of invitation from Osaka. The Governor, Mayor and a number of leading citizens asked us to come to their city as their guests for five days. They were joined by the governors of the neighbouring prefectures and the Mayors of Kyoto and Kobe, who together wanted to plan for a two-week programme in the Kansai area. The Kansai embraced the cultural heart of the country – Kyoto and Nara, the port city of Kobe and the bustling industries in and around Osaka. There was a joke, with a certain basis of truth, that the standard greeting of two Osaka businessmen was not 'Good Morning,' but 'How's Business?' Ken and I warmly accepted the invitation.

In the ten days before we left for Osaka we continued our rounds of interviews, meals, meetings and receptions with interesting personalities. The most dynamic was Ichiro Ishikawa, chairman of the most powerful business group, the Federation of Economic Organizations (*Keidanren*), who hosted a luncheon followed by a meeting for top industrialists. We also called on two men of prime importance in the news media – Tetsuo Furugaki, President of NHK, Japan National Radio (there was as yet no television), and George Togasaki, publisher of the *Nippon Times*, leading English language daily. Both offered their help in informing the public about MRA.

We had a memorable visit with one of the most respected couples in Japan, Prince and Princess Chichibu. The Prince, younger brother of the Emperor, was known internationally as a sports enthusiast and supporter of the Olympics, and a forward-looking man. The Princess, a commoner before her marriage, was the most gracious and outgoing of all the Imperial family. They had lived in retreat since the war in a cottage in the village of Gotemba at the foot of Mount Fuji. The prince was ill with tuberculosis and died not long after our visit. The Chichibus received us graciously, gave us a simple lunch and plied us with questions about the world, about MRA and about our time in Japan.

When our train pulled into Kyoto we were met by an official car of the neighbouring prefecture of Shiga and driven over a mountain pass to the town of Otsu on the shore of Lake Biwa. We had arrived in the heart of Japan's conservative countryside and the stronghold of her Buddhist traditions. Governor Hattori, our host, was a symbol of this past. At a time when almost all men wore Western-style business suits, he was wearing a kimono. That evening he entertained us at a lavish dinner, followed by a meeting with prefectural officials and civic leaders. The following morning we moved back several centuries during a visit to a Buddhist monastery on the top of Mount Hiye. For four hours Ken and I met with the presiding Abbot of the Tendai sect and his monks. Their sect had its strict disciplines and was dedicated to the precepts of 'Cold, Poverty, Debate and Hunger,' not exactly popular ideas in the modern world. We were called on to explain at length the basic philosophy of Moral Re-Armament and were given the Abbot's blessing on our work.

For five busy days in Osaka we were lunched, dined and asked to speak at meetings. We quickly sensed the enthusiastic spirit of the city, similar perhaps to that of Chicago, fiercely competitive with New York. Osaka, number two in Japan, appeared to be trying a little harder. Not least among the dynamic figures was our host, Governor Bunzo Akama, who personified the pragmatic, bustling outlook of the area. We were given reception-meetings by *Mainichi* and *Asahi*, the Osaka branch of the Bank of Japan, the Chamber of Commerce, the Economic Federation and the Governor and Mayor. We spoke at a public meeting sponsored by the Education Association to students of Osaka University, at a Rotary Club luncheon, and wound up at a conference of the top businessmen organized by Michisuke Sugi, head of the Chamber of Commerce.

Police Chief Eiji Suzuki arranged for Ken and me to speak to his 160 staff officers. This burly, even-tempered professional was one of the best-known and most capable figures in the police world. He gained national attention by his firm handling of Communist-inspired riots and violent demonstrations during the late 'forties. He also won high praise for cleaning up the city's formidable gangs of thugs and black marketeers.

As we entered the hall someone barked a command and all stood to attention as the Chief gave us a formal introduction. To break up the serious atmosphere of most Japanese meetings we often told jokes and made surprise remarks, and this occasion seemed to call for a special effort. Travelling with us was Sumi Mitsui's son Yori, a delightful young man who had grown up enjoying the amenities of life provided by an affluent family. When the Mitsuis, like the rest of the population, suffered privation at the end of the war, Yori set up a successful black market operation. Then, struck by his parents' sincere adherence to moral standards, he came clean with them. We introduced Yori to the audience and when he started telling them about his adventures and his change he grabbed their attention. His father followed him on the platform and described his family: 'I am a typical businessman – a coconut – you know, very hard outside, very soft inside. My wife is a typical Japanese woman – a peach – soft and beautiful outside, very hard inside.' He went on, 'My daughter is a chestnut – very prickly outside, and very hard inside.' By this time the police were laughing, nodding, relaxed.

Kyoto was the one large city in Japan which had been spared destruction by bombs and fire during the war. In a tacit agreement, the Japanese quartered no soldiers there and there were no significant arms plants. So the temples, shrines and gardens remained unspoiled. In the great temple, Higashi Honganji, headquarters of the Jodo Shinshu sect, with its millions of members across Japan, we were received at tea by the Chief Abbot Otani and his wife, a younger sister of the Empress. They pressed us with many questions about MRA and the response we had received and were especially interested in our visit to Mount Hiye. We learned of the centuries-old feud between these two main Buddhist sects: the Mount Hiye priests were looked on for many years as wild robber monks who pillaged other monasteries!

Then we were joined by Setsuo Yamada and taken by train along the beautiful Inland Sea shore to Hiroshima. Awaiting us at the station was a large group of journalists who called for a press conference on the spot. They fired the expected questions at us – 'Why have you come to Hiroshima?' 'What do you think of the dropping of the atom bomb?' 'What are your reactions to Japan?' Ken and I had talked over our apprehensions at visiting Hiroshima less than five years since the August morning when the bomb levelled the city. What kind of a reception could we as Americans expect from the survivors?

We were treated with consideration by the newspapermen and then driven with Yamada to stay at the home of a friend over-looking the waterfront at Miyajima Island as there was no suitable accommodation in the city. Next morning Mayor Hamai came to give us a warm greeting. During our four days with him we became impressed with his single-minded dedication to the rebuilding of Hiroshima. He told us he was deeply grateful for the material aid received from the United States towards the reconstruction, now two-thirds completed, of the homes and essential buildings of the city. He took us on a tour and we saw some of these buildings going up. Most looked flimsy, the whole area reminiscent of a hastily thrown up Western mining town.

Governor Tsunei Kusunose, who looked like a prosperous businessman, was quietly cordial. We went from his office to a luncheon given by the Chamber of Commerce and the Bankers Association. Then came a public meeting in the hall just a block from the building above which the bomb had exploded. The skeleton of its dome and walls was being preserved as a grim reminder of the tragedy. Ken and I said our lives were given to the task of rebuilding the world so that war became unthinkable. Peace, we believed, required that men and women and nations lived differently than in the past, freed from the greed, hatred and materialism which create conflict. America, perhaps as much as any country, needed change and certainly the Japanese, and especially the citizens of Hiroshima, who understood the cost of war, had a great part to play in helping to remake the world. There were many questions, reflecting no bitterness but a great desire to understand Moral Re-Armament, and among many a wish to have a part in it. After three hours Yamada brought the meeting to an end, but still many of the audience stayed on, talking with us. It was a moving and humbling experience.

We were taken to the Itsukaichi Orphanage, where children whose parents had died in the atomic explosion were cared for. Some had been terribly burned and crippled. Young girls presented us with bouquets of flowers and sang for us. We toured the Atomic Bomb Casualty Commission headquarters, an American organization founded for the study of long-term effects of radiation. The one strong note of criticism of America we heard was in connection with the ABCC. Some Japanese were understandably bitter because the institution was only authorized to research, not to give long-term medical treatment to the thousands who still suffered from the nuclear fall out.

From Hiroshima we travelled westwards to the island of Kyushu. Our first stop was at the naval base of Sasebo, hometown of Tokutaro Kitamura, a Diet member whom I had entertained in Washington, who was on hand to greet us. We journeyed on with him to Nagasaki, the other city hit by an atom bomb. Nagasaki had been the most international city in Japan, since this was the one base permitted for some centuries to Dutch and other foreign traders, when the country's rulers were determined to isolate Japan from the rest of the world. At the end of the sixteenth century the Catholic missionaries there were attacked for being too zealous and they and many of their Japanese converts were massacred. The Cathedral, which survived the atomic blast, is their memorial.

The Governor, Mayor, President of the City Council, President of the Prefectural Assembly and the civic leaders of several neighbouring towns were on hand to entertain us at dinner.

Then Kitamura rescued us from the non-stop activities and took us off to Unzen National Park, one of Japan's beauty spots. Volcanic springs bubble up from the hills, clouds of steam rise in the valleys and the hot water is piped into medicinal baths.

After two days there we set off by car and boat for Omuta, where the Mitsui Mining Company had its headquarters. Accompanied by Sumi Mitsui, we were assured of a royal welcome by the company officials of this largest coal-producing firm in Japan. We were taken down the Miike Mine, met with company officials and also with the officers of the miners' union. Although the working and living conditions were better than average in the coal industry, they were terrible by Western standards. Even before World War II there had been strikes and unrest and after the war, with the legalizing of labour unions, the Mitsui miners were prime targets for Marxist indoctrination. We had a lively time with the union leaders; some of them accused us of being tools of the capitalists. Noboru Agune, the young president of the union, was especially critical, but over a meal we moved to more positive ground. All agreed that changes were needed in capitalists and Communists alike in order to remake the world.

3

TIGER BY THE TAIL

As we rode the train back to Tokyo, a 30-hour journey, we talked about the past ten weeks. The countryside was ablaze with cherry blossoms and our mood matched the coming of spring. We were still a little dazed by the way we had been catapulted into a nation's life, the variety of the people we had met, and their energy, enthusiasm and response. We realized that while still self-critical and doubtful about Japan's future, people seemed to be coming to life and ready to make up their minds about the direction in which they wanted their country to go. They were still appreciative of America's generous material aid and bold reforms under the Occupation, but also starting to react against having to depend so heavily on a foreign power, and critical of the life-styles they saw in many American military personnel and traders. Ken and I had voiced confidence in Japan's future role in the world, affirmed the basic moral standards that most Japanese wanted to see re-established, and were honest about America's materialism and need for change. People in all sectors of life had seemed to respond to the challenge that they had a great part to play in remaking their country if they would pay the price in their own lives.

Most of those we had met were intensely curious about the outside world, from which Japan had been cut off since the war years. They wanted to know how other peoples were faring and to learn all they could from them. Most of all, they longed to travel and see for themselves – at that time an impossible dream. As Ken and I moved through the cities of the Kansai we had had the idea of mobilizing a delegation of Japanese representing various facets of national life to take part in the summer conference at Caux, and then travel through several countries, as the Katayamas had done the previous year.

We knew that we had been led to men who were already playing an influential role in running the country and we believed that, away from the demands of their work and in the perspective of the world which Caux offered, some of them might be further equipped to take on together the moral and spiritual direction of Japan.

At a conference of top businessmen in Osaka we launched this proposal and were startled by their enthusiastic response. When we arrived back in Tokyo we realized that in our innocence we had grabbed a tiger by the tail. On the one hand, we were being pressed by governors, mayors and leading citizens from Osaka, Kobe, Kyoto, Hiroshima and Nagasaki to be included in the delegation; on the other, we came face to face with a bewildering tangle of bureaucratic regulations. Our plan was simple in outline – select a delegation of about sixty, charter a plane to Geneva to arrive in mid-June at Caux, spend a couple of weeks there and then take the group through West Germany, Paris, London, and across the United States. We figured the minimum cost of this round-the-world tour at $2,000 per person, knowing that many of our MRA friends would gladly want to make sacrifices to meet some of the costs of hospitality and travel.

As soon as we approached the authorities – the Japanese Government, the military Occupation staff and the airlines – we were met with consternation and incredulity. They said we were asking for the travellers to be processed through military intelligence, visa requirements, foreign currency exchange permission – all in two months. That time was barely sufficient for clearance of one well qualified individual – as for sixty! The experts shook their heads and said they were glad they were not in our shoes.

A delicate aspect of the project was the selection of the best qualified candidates amidst the growing stream of applicants. To our small bedroom at the Teito Hotel came friends old and new – all with a burning interest, they said, in Moral Re-Armament! Governor Ichimada was enthusiastic about the project and we enlisted him and friends in the government, business and labour to help pick the right people. Ichimada went to work with top businessmen to encourage the best men to travel and also to provide funds for union leaders who were not able to finance themselves. Through Kitamura and Yamada we had sessions with the Speaker and President of the two Houses of the Diet to help choose the best representatives of the political parties. We also had conferences with top officials of the Finance and Labour Ministries and Occupation staff on how to tackle all the regulations. And we canvassed the airlines for the best offer for charters, which were in short supply.

After a few days we began to have a clearer picture of the dimensions and priorities of our undertaking and realized that the essential requirement was the fullest co-operation on the part of General MacArthur's staff. They would have to handle the bulk of the investigations and paper work and, most important of all, only they could authorize the exchange of Japanese yen into US dollars, which were required by the airlines. We had been sending reports of our activities to Colonel Nugent, and we consulted him about these key problems of clearance to leave the country and currency exchange. Nugent said he felt that now was the time for us to have a direct touch with General MacArthur, as only he could authorize the journey. A few days later he telephoned to say he had obtained an interview for us, adding that from the questions MacArthur had asked about our progress it was clear that he had read the reports we had sent through Nugent. He asked us to call on Colonel Bunker, the General's aide, for a briefing before the interview, and wished us luck.

Bunker was cordial and businesslike. He said the General was well informed about what we had been doing and then advised us on how to conduct ourselves with MacArthur. He said his chief liked first to talk at length to his visitors, and we should listen and only speak when MacArthur had finished. Unless he indicated earlier that the interview was at an end, we should leave after thirty minutes. Above all, we were not to raise the questions of yen-dollar exchange for our proposed trip. This was impossible and the General did not wish to discuss the matter. Ken and I felt we were being prepared for a reception by royalty. And in a sense we were: Douglas MacArthur, Supreme Commander of the Occupation Forces, was the most powerful man in Japan.

We were given a luncheon by Togasaki, publisher of *The Nippon Times*, and his staff. It proved to be a perfect prelude to our visit with MacArthur, who read the paper carefully. On the morning of the day we were to see him it carried an editorial about Moral Re-Armament in relation to Japan:

33

THE MRA IN JAPAN

The world-wide Moral Re-Armament (MRA) movement has come to Japan and is affording the Japanese people a chance to live and to practise the democracy which they now presumably follow. Democracy can become an even greater force for good in Japan as in other nations if the people translate into action what is now too often mere lip service.

MRA works on the simplest of formulas. Its basis is the individual – from all walks of life and from any nation. He is asked to observe in his daily activities the basic tenets of honesty, purity, unselfishness and love. His spiritual regeneration will affect and influence others around him and by spreading from one person to another permeate and move a whole nation.

The aim of MRA is to build a new world based upon unity and peace. It is the antithesis to the theory that human nature cannot be changed and therefore wars are inevitable. MRA is proving that human nature can be changed, and as the individual changes so can the family, the community and the nation.

MRA thus has a real message for Japan as it has for the world. It is pointing the way for the Japanese people to change themselves from their past role as a warlike people. It's affording a real opportunity to show through action that the Japanese people as a whole have experienced a spiritual awakening and have finally overcome their unsavoury reputation of the past.

If Japan can honestly repent her past misdeeds against her neighbours and can show a sincerity of purpose to work unselfishly in the interest of world peace, the struggle to overcome the distrust and suspicion felt against her will be more than half won. Indeed, the spread of MRA through Japan – in every phase of her activities – would represent a final crystallization of the great transformation this nation has undergone under the wise tutelage of the Occupation.

Douglas MacArthur had become a larger-than-life sized legend in post-war Japan, rivalling the Emperor as a father figure in the eyes of millions of Japanese. Terrified at the prospect of cruel reprisals at the hands of the American military, they had been surprised by the discipline and even-handed conduct of the troops under MacArthur's command. The constitutional reforms, including releasing of political prisoners, legalization of labour unions, revival of democratic institutions, land reform and universal suffrages were accepted by most Japanese, who regarded the Supreme Commander as their author.

The General had carefully cherished the image of a stern disciplinarian, a dashing soldier and a benign statesman. His open-necked khaki shirt and corn-cob pipe were symbols of his no-nonsense democratic posture. Four times a day, at the same hours, he entered and left the doors of his headquarters to salutes of a highly polished, beautifully drilled honour guard. The spectacle drew as many onlookers as does the Changing of the Guard at Buckingham Palace.

When Ken and I were ushered into his office MacArthur greeted us warmly. He looked exactly like his pictures – tall, trim and aquiline. After a firm handshake he motioned us to armchairs, lighted up his celebrated pipe and proceeded to do the exact opposite of everything his aide had predicted. Settling back, he said, 'I want to hear about your time in Japan and what conclusions you have come to about the country.' We said we had only been there ten weeks and did not regard ourselves as authorities on Japan. He laughed and said, yes, it was only during the first ten days that Americans felt they knew all there was to know about the country. We described some of our experiences and told him of the response we were getting to the proposal to take a top level delegation to Europe and the United States.

'Yes, I've heard about that, and I think it's an excellent idea to expose selected men and women to the best that the West can show them. I understand that you are experiencing difficulties in securing dollars and have raised the question of converting yen to dollars. I wish I could help; however, we have had to establish very strict currency regulations and I'm sorry it isn't possible to make an exception.' He asked how we were supported financially, and when we told him it was basically through the sacrificial giving by thousands of people he wanted to know why Rockefeller, Ford and Carnegie monies were not behind us. Then he smiled and said he himself had failed to get funds from these sources for his projects.

As we talked more about some of the people we had met he commented that we had made an unusually wide range of contacts.

He added, 'I am deeply in sympathy with the basic concepts of your work.' He talked about the failure of character to keep pace with knowledge and spoke of the need for leadership and the difficulty of raising it up in any country. 'In America it is especially difficult, because of the newspaper columnists whose livelihood is character assassination. First they destroy a man's confidence in himself and then they destroy the public's confidence in him.'

Towards the end of our conversation the General talked about the threat to East Asia posed by the victory of the Communists in mainland China. 'Formosa is now a point of vital concern. Have you considered going there? You should.' We told him of an invitation from General Ho Ying-chin, Governor Wu and others, and that we planned to leave Tokyo early next morning for twelve days on the island of Formosa (Taiwan). He asked us to give his personal greetings to Generalissimo and Madame Chiang Kai-shek. We left after forty minutes of conversation which impressed us with MacArthur's deep concern for the future of that part of the world, for which he felt very much responsible. We felt that Japan had been extremely fortunate to come under his control, to benefit from the security, material aid and firm framework of democracy which the Occupation provided while the country staggered to its feet and took stock of its resources and its future.

The dozen days we spent in Taiwan were exhilarating, but did not bear directly on our efforts in Japan. We were house guests of General Ho, former Prime Minister and Chief of Staff and later of Taiwan's Governor Wu, and they opened every door to us. President and Madame Chiang Kai-shek invited us for lunch at their villa outside Taipei. Most of our conversation with them was about the perilous state of Taiwan in the face of Communist China and their urgent need for military supplies from the United States, which the Truman administration was denying them. Among others with whom we talked were Prime Minister Cheng Chen and several members of the Cabinet, and many of the military top brass, including General Sun Li-jen, Commander of the Ground Forces. He asked us to address a training class for generals. We also found ourselves inspecting army, navy and air force facilities.

When Ken and I returned to Tokyo in early May a procession of governors, mayors, Diet Members and businessmen besieged us. Each was accompanied by a secretary who carried a large bundle of yen, the equivalent of the $2,000 for the trip. Rumours reached us of feuds within the political parties as to who should be allowed to go to Caux. So we obtained an interview with Prime Minister Yoshida to inform him about our plans and ask his help. He applauded our efforts to take a group to Europe and approved of the selection of two members of his party, Chojiro Kuriyama and Tokoyasu Fukuda, who had approached us as candidates. We also talked with Yoshida about our problem of exchanging yen for dollars. He was sympathetic, but said if MacArthur did not approve it, there was nothing to be done. But he would work to see if there was some way to apply pressure at Cabinet level. The Cabinet decided to ask MacArthur for permission to exchange $20,000's worth of yen, but after some debate at high levels, the request was turned down. We were finally able to secure the dollars we needed four days before departure as a gift from Jack and Connie Ely, Washington friends who were associated with MRA. Meantime, spurred by directives from the top, Foreign Office officials and Occupation staff laboured heroically to complete security checks and travel documents for all the travellers.

At the last moment Katsuji Nakajima, the militant labour leader whom we had met in Ueda, came to see us. Something powerful was at work in his mind and heart. He told us he and his wife had found that a Communist colleague in his town was having trouble in his marriage and had decided to separate from his wife. After talking with the Nakajimas he and his wife had stayed together and he resigned from the Party because he realized his political activities were endangering his marriage. When we told Nakajima that funds had been given to cover his expenses for the trip, he accepted our invitation to join the delegation.

On June 12, our last day in Japan and my 39th birthday, Ken and I were invited to luncheon by the Prime Minister. He included some of the Cabinet and senior men in our delegation. Yoshida rose at the end of the meal and addressed the company. He gave a striking evaluation of the mission on which his countrymen were embarking. 'In 1870 a representative group of Japanese travelled to the West. On their return they changed the course of Japanese life. I believe that when this delegation returns, you, too, will open a new page in our history.' The group last century had gone under the orders of the Emperor Meiji to learn the secret of industrialization. The result of their mission was the opening of Japan to modern industry and business and to propel it into the nineteenth century.

Late that evening the travellers assembled at Haneda airport, accompanied by a far greater crowd of family and friends who had come to bid them farewell. Among the sixty were seven prefectural governors, including several of national stature; senior Diet Members representing all the major parties; top level industrial, banking and labour leaders; and the mayors of four cities, including Hiroshima and Nagasaki. In the party were seven wives – it was almost unheard of for the Japanese to be accompanied by their wives on any kind of business. And accompanying the delegation were our stalwart friends the Mitsuis and Sohmas, a young woman, Toneko Kimura, who had travelled with us as secretary and interpreter, and was to give years of unstinting service, Sen Nishi-yama, a brilliant interpreter, who obtained leave from the American Embassy, and several other young people who would serve as aides and interpreters.

Normally there was no occasion which could draw together such diverse elements of Japanese society, still divided by class distinctions and conflicting political and economic objectives. There was another aspect of the delegation which was much on our minds as the mission set off. Its members were leaving the country less than five years after its surrender in World War II. No peace treaty had yet been signed and the Japanese were technically enemies of countries they were about to enter. The bitter hurts and hates caused by the Japanese military were still vivid in the hearts of some whom they would be meeting.

Our charter plane's first stop would be Manila, the plane's home base, where it would be fuelled before taking off across Asia. No Japanese had yet been allowed to set foot in the Philippines because of the cruelties of the Japanese occupation. The airline officials had strongly advised us to make sure that none of the delegation strayed away from the lounge where they would be looked after while the plane was being serviced. Otherwise, they warned, the company could not be held responsible for any 'unfortunate incidents'.

As our DC-6 roared down the runway and lifted off over a moonlit Tokyo Bay, Ken and I marvelled at the miracles beyond our powers which had made this venture possible, shook a little in our shoes at the foolhardiness of undertaking it, and breathed a prayer to the Almighty that the promise of the mission would be fulfilled.

4

MISSION TO THE WEST

Our plane touched down at Manila's airport on a steaming June
morning. As the delegates walked into the terminal building, we
saw some Filipinos eyeing them suspiciously. Ken and I prowled
around like watchdogs during the three hours we were on the
ground, discouraging our Japanese friends from wandering away.
Many of them were eager photographers, enticed into detours by
arresting sights; others just liked to go their own way at their own
pace. This was the first of hundreds of occasions during the next
few weeks when we were counting heads and making sure that
nobody was left behind.

The following day, after refuelling stops in Calcutta, Karachi,
Tel Aviv and Rome, our DC-6 arrived at the Geneva airport and
a weary delegation trooped into chartered buses for the last leg of
the journey. We drove along Lake Leman's north shore through
ancient towns and villages, catching glimpses of Mont Blanc,
gleaming pink in the late afternoon sunshine. Ahead, the dramatic
profile of the Dents du Midi swung into view, above the Rhone
Valley.

In Montreux we left the lake and began the steep, zig-zag climb
up the mountain slopes to Caux, perched half way up to the rocky
summit of the Rochers-de-Naye. As the buses swung around the
last few hairpin bends, the turrets and balconies of Mountain
House loomed above us. The travellers, many of whom had been
dozing, came to life and oohed and aahed at the imposing scene.
Our cavalcade came around the corner of the building and there,
lining the walls and front entrance, were several hundred people,
many in national costumes, waving and cheering. Frank Buchman
had planned an all-out welcome for the Japanese. With the
representatives of many countries, he awaited them at the doors of

41

the large circular lobby and greeted each one personally, as they were introduced.

This welcome and the atmosphere of friendliness with which they were surrounded during the following days took the Japanese by surprise. Along with their eagerness to associate with foreigners, they dreaded the reactions they might meet. One of the labour leaders, Daiji Ioka, Chairman of the Municipal Workers of Osaka, expressed the feeling of some of his countrymen when he spoke to the assembly: 'Our nation took a road to war which has caused tremendous suffering to the world. When my colleagues and I left Tokyo we fully expected to be treated as enemies, even to the point of segregation, but we were overwhelmed by the warmth of the welcome we received.'

During the next couple of weeks the Japanese met the citizens of close to fifty countries. They heard former enemies – French and German, bosses and workers, Communists and anti-Communists, Christians and Moslems – tell of dramatic reconciliations with each other. They took meals with husbands and wives, and parents and children who had been reunited, and talked with people from many walks of life who had found an answer to hatred, bitterness and jealousies. All this had its impact on the delegation, some of whom were not on speaking terms with each other when they stepped onto the plane in Tokyo.

One of the first who publicly expressed a change of attitude towards an enemy was Mayor Matsuhashi of Nagano City. Speaking from the platform he said, 'About three years ago, when Mr Hayashi became Governor of Nagano, I was Speaker of the Prefectural Assembly. I gave my approval to things which I thought were good for the prefecture, but I also had great bitterness to Mr Hayashi . . . I have now apologized to him. From now on I want to work together with him for the good of the prefecture and city as a true friend.'

Governor Hayashi stood beside the Mayor and took up the story: 'Mr Matsuhashi and I have been political enemies. We two came together here at Caux, grasped each other's hands and committed ourselves to establish a sound statesmanship, not only for our prefecture, but in Japan, on the basis of not *who*, but *what* is right. This is one of the great gifts we will take back from Caux.'

An even more dramatic reconciliation came a few days later. On the plane, Katsuji Nakajima, the young militant labour leader, had been shocked to find Eiji Suzuki as a fellow passenger. He regarded the Osaka police chief as public enemy number one, because of the forceful measures he had used in quelling disturbances. During some sleepless nights at Caux he looked hard and long at his hatred of the man. Finally, he felt impelled to go to Suzuki's room and ask to talk to him. The young man told him he did not share the police chief's political or economic views, but felt his hatred towards Suzuki was wrong. He wanted to leave it behind and asked Eiji to forgive him. Both men were moved to tears. Next day they spoke together from the platform and pledged to work together for national unity.

Another effect of the assembly on the Japanese was a reorienting of priorities in their private lives and in public policy. Tokutaro Kitamura, for example, who had served as Minister of Finance, told the assembly, 'We are the thirtieth country in the world in area and the sixth in population, and only 15.5% of the area is arable. Of all those working in Japan, 53% are in agriculture. Over 120 cities have been burnt down. Out of this great loss during the war we must build up a new economy in our nation. But a far more serious task is the moral rehabilitation of the nation. We have discovered that the spirit we have found here in Caux is the road we can go to rebuild morality in the nation and also in its economic structure.'

Chojiro Kuriyama, who had been asked by the Prime Minister to be his personal representative on the Mission, told the conference, 'When we hear of absolute honesty all of us Japanese are heavily jolted. We think about our tax system and wonder if it would be possible to have enough left for the barest living expenses if we paid all our taxes honestly. However, we have people here who could do something – an ex-Finance Minister and six Members of the Diet, including a Socialist Member who is a financial authority. We ought at least to do everything possible to establish a tax system which will make it possible for honest payment of taxes.'

Another Member of the Diet, who had been included in the group at the last moment, was Yasuhiro Nakasone. During the conference he confided to me, 'I am the youngest Diet Member, and I am going to become Prime Minister.' A little more than thirty years later, he was to achieve his goal. While at Caux he wrote an article for a home town newspaper, describing perhaps the most important change of attitude among members of the delegation – a re-evaluation of their acceptance of class-war and confrontation in industry as the only road to travel. He reported, 'People who spoke at the assembly were largely representatives of labour and management from various countries. The thing that drew our greatest interest was the fact that many Communists from the Ruhr coal mines of Germany and the longshoremen's union of England have changed their way of thinking and are now becoming passionate, moving forces for this new programme in these same areas. . . . The Japanese representatives who heard these witnesses had many doubts and conflicts within their hearts. Some of the excuses they made were: "The workers of Japan are up against a far more serious problem of living which will not permit such sweet compromises; we have to solve first the problem of our inadequate national resources." However, the ice in the Japanese hearts was melted by the international harmony that transcends race and class in this great current of world history moving through the continents of America and Europe.'

On June 25, the North Korean Army launched a surprise attack across the 38th Parallel into South Korea. Next day, the United Nations Security Council condemned the invasion as aggression and ordered the North Korean force to withdraw. On the following day, President Truman sent US forces into action to enforce UN orders. But the invaders swept southwards and a full scale war started. The news electrified the Japanese delegation. To Europeans, the fighting lay half across the world, but the shores of Japan and Korea are only a hundred miles apart, and thousands of Koreans, sympathetic to North Korea, were a disruptive force living in Japan. As the Communists pushed rapidly southward the Japanese asked Ken and me to meet with them. Should they return? Some of them, especially the governors, felt they should be home, reassuring their citizens and dealing with any emergencies. Others were undecided. We urged not taking any hasty action, and the delegation finally decided to suspend making any move, and in a few days some of them received reassuring letters from their people, advising them to continue their journey. The intervention by MacArthur's seasoned troops did something to relieve the panic.

The news of the fighting also forced the Japanese to examine their attitude to war in general. The bitter experiences of World War II had made most Japanese emotionally allergic to involvement in any war. It had been only too easy for them to accept the ban on military forces which had been written into the constitution at the insistence of the United States. They were now counting on Americans for defence, should their country be attacked. For their own part, they wanted to remain neutral and uncommitted. There were even powerful voices being raised in Japan against permitting the country to be used as a military arsenal and a base to stem the North Korean invasion. However, the Japanese came to appreciate the UN and US intervention in a desperate situation. Later, they went on record that they approved Japan's whole-hearted economic support of the military sanctions.

The delegates were anxious to see as much of Switzerland as they could – the beautiful countryside, the cities, the industries and the Swiss way of life. It was popular in Japan to refer to their country as 'the Switzerland of Asia,' a phrase used by MacArthur. By this was meant not only the similarity of their alpine splendours, but also that post-war Japan emulated the rugged reputation for neutrality which the Swiss enjoyed. The delegates received a shock when we took them on a tour of central Switzerland and they learned that every able-bodied Swiss had to take rigorous military training and was then placed on the active reserve, with regular periodic training and on call for immediate duty in emergency. Even more surprising to them, every man was armed with a rifle which he kept ready in his home. The Swiss, they discovered, did not equate neutrality with pacifism.

Their tour included a visit to Berne, where leaders of the delegation were received by Max Petitpierre, the President. The Mayors of Geneva, Zurich and Berne gave them receptions. In Geneva the President of the International Red Cross welcomed them. They toured the largest industrial plants, Sulzer, Brown Boveri and Escher Wyss, and were entertained by both directors and union leaders.

Before they boarded a plane for West Germany Frank Buchman took them to see the house in Zurich where his ancestor, Bibliander, a colleague of Zwingli, the Protestant reformer, had lived. Then he stood, bowing at the plane ramp, as his guests, bowing in return, filed into the plane. It was a typical gesture of a sensitive host, who had a remarkable way of entering into the minds and hearts of all manner of people.

The delegation flew into Duesseldorf, where the Lord Mayor and a group of city officials met the plane and took the guests for lunch. Kitamura and Governor Akama replied to the Mayor's address of welcome, saying they had found at Caux the basis for peace, unity and international understanding and trade. Their speeches, together with an interview with the Mayor of Hiroshima, were reported widely and broadcast across the country.

That afternoon I escorted fifteen of the Japanese to Bonn for an interview with Konrad Adenauer, the German Chancellor. Adenauer, who was to become the outstanding European politician during the 'fifties and 'sixties, had visited Caux the previous summer. We were ushered into his spacious office and I introduced each of the Japanese, saying a little about each one. Adenauer shook hands with them and asked them to be seated. He told them what a great pleasure it was to receive such a distinguished delegation.

'I know Caux well,' he told them. 'Dr Buchman is making a great contribution to international unity and to the establishment of social justice.' He expressed his appreciation of MRA and went on to speak of the problems facing Germany, especially its division between East and West, and said it was his conviction that ultimately Germany would be reunited. Kuriyama responded with greetings from Frank Buchman and Prime Minister Yoshida and said the delegation had found at Caux the key to the future of Japan. Adenauer asked for further news of what they had seen at Caux, and Kitamura spoke up about the grave economic problems of Japan, but said they had discovered at Caux that economic and financial stability depended on spiritual and moral change and that they were returning to fight for Moral Re-Armament in their country. He added that they wanted to fight shoulder to shoulder with Germany in the remaking of the world. After half an hour they all marched down the stairs in front of the cameras, shook hands and talked together.

Ninety pressmen, including representatives of world news agencies, were assembled in the press centre of the Parliament building. A lively question-and-answer session was followed by individual interviews and broadcasts by Kuriyama and Mayor Hamai, beamed to East and West Germany. Then we drove back to the Ruhr to join the delegation at a dinner given by the Lord Mayor of Essen. Next day the party split up – eighteen drove to Hamburg and Bremen for a top-level programme arranged in those two port cities by their Lord Mayors; eleven flew to West Berlin at the invitation of that city; and the main party stayed in the Ruhr for a programme of visits through coal mines, factories and housing estates. I flew with the group to Berlin.

It was not until ten years later that the Communists sealed off East Berlin and East Germany with the Wall, but barbed wire and armed guards between the East and West Occupation Zones in Berlin made it clear that the ideological frontier was already a grim reality. West Berlin, controlled by the Americans, British and French, was a democratic island in Russian-controlled East Germany. Its mayor, Ernst Reuter, veteran Socialist, symbolized the city's rugged defiance of Communism. He and his City Council entertained the Japanese at an impressive luncheon. As the visitors arrived outside the City Hall they saw two enormous flags, German and Japanese, hanging above the entrance. Under MacArthur's Occupation policies it was forbidden to fly the Japanese flag, and when the Japanese saw their national banner, tears came to their eyes.

In the Lord Mayor's office the party was surrounded by what one official said was the largest battery of newsreel, radio and newspaper men he had ever seen there. The visitors signed the Golden Book, reserved for VIPs, and Mayor Hamai presented Reuter with a small cross carved from the wood of an ancient camphor tree which had stood immediately below the Hiroshima bomb blast. Photos of the event were carried on the front page of many German newspapers next day, together with Hamai's words to Reuter, 'I hope the citizens of Berlin will join with the citizens of Hiroshima in fighting to build a new world in the spirit of Caux.'

At the luncheon which followed, Kitamura enlarged on that conviction in the closing words of his speech: 'The most serious fact today is that the world is now two and not one. After coming here to Berlin, where this division is such a grim reality, one feels all the more need for some unifying principle. There must be a new crusade for freedom and truth and we feel that the German and Japanese people should work together for it. I am fully convinced that Moral Re-Armament is the way this crusade can best be developed, and that is why we Japanese came to Caux to be trained in this ideology.'

It was fascinating to watch how determinedly many of the Japanese were making use of the discoveries they had made at Caux. Governor Hayashi, for example, created great interest by relating the story of the conservative Mayor of Nagano apologizing to him and deciding not to oppose him in the next elections for governor. He said he was particularly glad to tell this as a Socialist to fellow Socialists. In Japan their party had too many divisions and must find a new unity.

In Bonn, the US High Commissioner, John McCloy, who was in charge of the American Occupation Zone, gave a reception at which he made an impromptu speech. He told them that as Assistant Secretary of War, he and Secretary Stimson had made the decision to save Kyoto from bombing. Kuriyama replied, expressing his country's gratitude to America for all the Occupation was doing for Japan, and went on to say they had come to Caux for ideological training in basic moral and spiritual values.

The President of the Lower House and the Vice-President of the Upper House welcomed the party in the Parliament Buildings. Several of the labour and Socialist delegates had forty minutes with Dr Kurt Schumacher, Leader of the Opposition. At the end of this time, Socialist Diet Member Kawashima topped off the discussion by saying, 'Since coming to Caux we Japanese Socialists have seen how we lost our position as the Government party because we were not morally sound. I have concluded that, important as social and economic reconstruction are, they are of no use without the fundamental moral and spiritual basis which MRA provides.' Schumacher responded candidly, 'Well, that is where we in Germany also have not yet found a full solution.' The busy day ended with a dinner given by the Federal Government and chaired by Vice-Chancellor Bluecher.

Next morning they flew to Paris and were plunged into a press conference at Orly airport. Kuriyama set the keynote in his statement: 'Japan has suffered greatly for having followed a false ideology. Our task now is to rebuild our nation on the basis of

Chancellor Konrad Adenauer welcomes members of the Japanese party visiting Europe in 1950. Left to right: Tokuyasu Fukuda, Liberal Party; Ri Aoki, Governor of the Prefecture of Mie; Katsuji Nakajima, Executive of Metal Workers Union; Yasuhiru Nakasone, Democratic Party; Dr Adenauer (seated)

The Lord Mayor of London, Sir Frederick Rowland receives a wooden cross from the Mayor of Hiroshima, Shinzo Hamai, in the Mansion House. The cross was carved from a 400-year-old camphor tree planted at the founding of the city and blasted by the atom bomb.

Yokio Ozaki, 'Father' of the
Japanese Diet, with his
daughter Yukika Sohma in
America, 1950

U.S. Vice-President Barkley,
with Senator H. Alexander
Smith (left), receives the
Japanese Delegation of 1950 to
Congress. Representative
Tokutaro Kitamura (third from
right) addressed the House of
Representatives, Chojiro
Kuriyama (second from right)
spoke to the Senate.

that moral ideology which is at the heart of true democracy.' They went at once to a reception at the National Assembly given by Members of the Chamber of Deputies, and to another one at the Quai d'Orsay, given by the Foreign Office. During three days in Paris the Japanese were entertained at a formal reception by the Mayor and some had long conferences with the Ministers of Reconstruction and Labour. The first full day was July 14, Bastille Day, and the delegation was welcomed to the official enclosure of President Auriol to watch the colourful parade.

Next stop was London. As I had discovered the year before with the Katayamas, the British were cautious in receiving their former enemies – the hurts of the war still too vivid. In Germany the Japanese had been greeted as fellow sufferers and victims of the war. But there was another major difference: the regular press and radio coverage in Germany and France had been not only extensive, but remarkable in its perception of the aims of the Japanese mission. The British media were much more concerned with kimonos and chopsticks and almost totally uninterested in what the visitors had to say about their country, ideology and the world.

Nevertheless, the six days in Britain were filled with worthwhile events as well as sightseeing. The Lord Mayor of London gave a formal reception at the Mansion House and there were similar occasions in Oxford, provided by the Mayor and the Vice-Chancellor of the University. The delegation was entertained at a tea party in the House of Lords to meet Members of both Houses. Smaller groups met with senior officers at the Foreign Office and with the editorial staff of *The Times*. The most lively event was a public meeting in the Town Hall of West Ham, a part of London known as the cradle of the British Labour Movement. The hall was designed to seat 900, but somehow 1500 squeezed in and gave the Japanese a standing ovation.

Before their departure for New York the delegates issued a statement to the press: 'We came to Europe, where Communism began, to find a positive answer to Communism. We found it at Caux, Switzerland, in the ideology of Moral Re-Armament. This way of life is in our opinion the essential basis for a solution to the problems facing us in Asia, and our gratitude goes to Dr Buchman and his fellow workers who are its pioneers. We are also grateful to the people of Europe for the warmth of their welcome. We realize that in the past Japan has caused great suffering to them through her pursuit of false ideas and false roads. We hope in the future as a nation to show by our deeds that we have found a change of heart and that we can make our contribution to the remaking of the world.'

The constant emphasis on ideology and Communism was a reflection of the times. The summer of 1950 was flawed by the violent attack by the North Koreans and, behind their arms, the looming menace of Red China. In Eastern Europe Russia was making theatening noises and tightening its hold on the Iron Curtain countries. In the United States the long drawn out trial of Alger Hiss for perjury had brought the issue of Communist conspiracy to the breakfast tables of millions. And Senator McCarthy had launched his ideological witch hunts, which shocked the country in the era of the Cold War.

The highlight of a busy schedule in New York was a visit to the United Nations, then headquartered at Lake Success on Long Island. They were received by the long-time General Secretary Trygve Lie, who gave the Japanese the first invitation their country had received to join the United Nations, from which they were at the moment excluded until a peace treaty was signed. Kitamura replied, saying that 'the Japanese people here present are very deeply convicted by a sense of responsibility and shame for the troubles they have created in the Far East, but we are especially grateful for the rapid action that has been taken by the United Nations for preserving the peace.'

On the first full day in Washington there were three major events – a reception in the US Senate, a Congressional lunch and a State Department reception. At each of these occasions members of the delegation had the opportunity to speak as representatives of their country to government and political leaders of America, and through the press to its people. It was the first time since the war that any such events had taken place. The stage had been set several days earlier by Senator Alexander Smith, who had obtained the agreement of his fellow Senators to have the delegation officially welcomed, when speaking about the visit during a debate in the Senate:

'Members on both sides of the aisle have voiced the need for a moral mobilization, a Marshall Plan of ideas, a Voice of America which is really strong enough to win the battle for the minds and hearts of men. We are spending many thousands of dollars a year for that purpose in Asia alone, but here in this chamber we are going to have a chance to do first-hand what can never be done so effectively over five thousand miles of ocean. These men can take back to the wide cross-section of Japan which they represent the conviction and impression of what we are striving to maintain and preserve in the world.'

When the delegates, looking a little apprehensive, arrived on Capitol Hill they were escorted up the steps of Congress and into the office of the Vice-President, Senator Alben Barkley of Kentucky. He greeted each one personally and led the Diet Members to seats on the floor of the Senate, while the rest were taken to the Diplomatic Gallery. He then introduced the delegates to the Senators and spoke about the long friendship between the United States and Japan which had been temporarily broken. He expressed the hope that this friendship 'may not only be resumed but may be permanent in status between the two countries.' Then two Democrats and two Republicans spoke – Tom Connally, Chairman of the Foreign Relations Committee, and Ralph Flanders of Vermont, Willis Robertson of Virginia, and Alex Smith. Barkley then invited Chojiro Kuriyama, as a representative of the Prime Minister, to address the Senate. Sen Nishiyama translated, as he continued to do so well through many demanding events.

Kuriyama began: 'It is our sincere regret that Japan has broken an almost century-old friendship between our two countries. In spite of this big mistake on our part, the magnanimous forgiveness and generosity of America not only allowed Japan to survive but is helping her recovery. . . .

'The lawless aggression in Korea is again involving America in great sacrifices. We Japanese wholeheartedly support the action taken by the United Nations and pay high respect to the courageous leadership of President Truman in this matter. I hope that Japan will be shown ways in which she can be of assistance in co-operation with the United States.

'Mr President, we went to Caux, Switzerland, in search of the true content of democracy. We found the ideology which will truly feed democracy in Japan, and at the same time which is the powerful answer to Communism. Now we are here to study the heritage of Great America. It will be a great happiness to the people in Japan if we can reconstruct our nation on the same principles.'

The New York Times referred to Kuriyama's apology and editorialized:

'All this in Washington, DC, a little less than four years after the atomic bombs fell on Hiroshima and Nagasaki. . . . The mayors of Hiroshima and Nagasaki were among today's visitors. If they, too, felt that they had something to forgive they had achieved that miracle. For a moment we could see out of the present darkness into the years when all men may become brothers.'

Another editorial in the popular magazine *Saturday Evening Post*, quoted from Kuriyama's speech and stressed his apology. It concluded:

'Difficult as it is for a "my country right or wrong" American to understand this kind of mental going-on, the idea of a nation admitting that it could be mistaken about anything has a refreshing impact. Perhaps it has a practical side too. Already most of us feel somewhat softer toward Japan than we swore on a stack of Bibles we ever would feel. Perhaps even Americans could think up a few past occasions of which it could be safely admitted, "We certainly fouled things up that time." '

At a luncheon given in the District of Columbia Committee Room and attended by a number of Senators and Representatives some of the Japanese had an opportunity to speak and answer questions. Congressman Preston of Georgia called it 'the most interesting and inspiring experience of my entire career in Washington.' Then the delegation trooped out onto the steps of the Capitol Building for photographs with many of their Congressional hosts.

From Capitol Hill they drove to Prospect House, the official residence of the State Department for entertaining guests. On the lawns of the Georgetown mansion, with views across the Potomac, the Japanese were greeted by their hosts – John Foster Dulles, then special adviser to the President; Dean Rusk, then Deputy Under

Secretary of State, and others. To meet the Japanese they had invited a cross-section of Washington's leadership, including Congressmen and representatives of many national organizations.

On the last full day in Washington the House of Representatives followed the example of the Senate. For the first time in its history the House received a foreign delegation on its floor. Majority Leader John McCormack and Minority Leader Joseph Martin escorted the Diet Members down the aisle and they were given a standing ovation as they were welcomed by Speaker Rayburn. He then invited Tokutaro Kitamura to the rostrum to address the House. As a representative of the Japanese people Kitamura apologized for 'the tragic trouble that we have caused to the people of the United States.'

Sitting in the gallery were members of a Parliamentary delegation from Australia on their way to Caux. Kitamura looked up at them and added his deepest regret for what Japan had done to Australia. His speech was interrupted several times by loud applause and at the close the Congressmen and spectators in the galleries rose in a prolonged ovation. One of the Australians, speaking later at Caux, said: 'We saw the spokesman for the Japanese nation apologize for the wrongs, suffering and the heartbreak Japan had caused. There was a hush, the most intense silence I have ever encountered. . . . It was history being made. We from Australia realized that in our global problems in the South Pacific we had only looked to our mother country, Britain, and to the United States for assistance – but now we had a third partner in terms of Pacific global strategy.'

In Los Angeles the delegation faced a group of pressmen who peppered them with questions ranging from use of the atomic bomb to their attitude towards the Korean War. By now most were seasoned spokesmen, able to field difficult questions and return shrewd replies. While in the city, the Japanese were entertained one day at the largest picnic I had ever seen. It was held in Elysian Park, sponsored by Japanese American communities from all over Southern California. The event symbolized a reunion between Japanese Americans and their kinsmen across the Pacific, cut off from each other by the war for nearly ten years. There were close to ten thousand men, women and children, eating hot dogs and water melon, running around, shouting and having a good time.

Then they sat quietly under the trees and listened to the travellers talking over a public address system.

Sunday, August 6, was the fifth anniversary of Hiroshima Day, and CBS had approached us with a proposal that Mayor Hamai should be interviewed with an interpreter over their radio network for thirty minutes. (Television was fast developing, but radio was still the mass medium.) Hamai agreed and we worked out with CBS a programme originating from MRA headquarters in Los Angeles to include not only the Mayor, but also Kuriyama, Dr Rufus Kleinsmid, Chancellor of the University of Southern California, Mayor Fletcher Bowron of Los Angeles, and Governor Earl Warren, later to become Chief Justice of the Supreme Court. The Governor would speak from Sacramento and the rest would take part in an official dinner given by the city.

Yukika Sohma was introduced as the daughter of elder statesman Ozaki. She gave a brilliant resumé of the mission to the West, and went on: 'The world does not look to America only for material aid, but also for spiritual leadership with the greatest confidence that in her spiritual heritage she has answers to bring unity to the now divided world. We are so grateful to you for bringing Moral Re-Armament to Japan. It is interpreting your great spiritual heritage of making democracy work in a way that anyone in Japan can understand. We women of Japan wish to do our best to bring this spirit to our country and through her change to the world, because we believe this is the only expression of restitution for her past wrongs, and with this ideology we can build a new world.'

Mayor Shinzo Hamai thanked Americans for their material and moral support in the reconstruction of his city. He recalled the horrors of the day five years ago when more than 100,000 lives were snuffed out. 'We people of Hiroshima,' he continued, 'hold no bitterness towards anyone because we have realized that this tragedy is naturally to be expected from war. The only thing we ask of the world is that everybody becomes aware of what happened in Hiroshima, how and why it happened, and exerts every effort to see it will not have to happen again in any other place. . . . We need to remove the boundary lines we have wilfully drawn in our hearts – the lines of race, nationality and class. They can be removed by a change of heart. . . . Dr Buchman has said, "Peace is people becoming different." This hits the nail on the head. I, for

54

one, intend to start this effort from Hiroshima. The one dream and hope left to our surviving citizens is to re-establish the city as a pattern for peace.'

The last stop in the journey was San Francisco. At a final meeting many of the delegation spoke briefly about their experiences and expressed their gratitude for what it had meant to them personally and as representatives of Japan. Several themes ran through what they said: the impact on their lives of the upbeat challenging atmosphere at Caux, where they had seen that dedicated men and women could bring positive changes in society; the stimulus of re-entering the community of nations, apologizing for their past and establishing bonds of friendship; the reordering of priorities in their personal, domestic and civic responsibilities – particularly a new emphasis on moral standards, rather than on material incentives.

On the morning of August 16, as the Japanese gathered at the airport for their flight home, they issued to the press a statement summarizing their convictions:

'We are returning to Japan to build there a citadel of inspired democracy under the wise leadership of General MacArthur. We deeply appreciate his great work in Japan and wish to support by every permissible means the courageous and sacrificial action of President Truman and the American people, under the flag of the United Nations, to protect our common freedoms. Our great desire is to make amends for our mistakes of the past by constituting our country a trusted partner of the United States in building a regenerated Asia.

'We came to the West in search of a new ideology which might fill the vacuum of belief among non-communist countries of the East. We found a vital answer at the World Assembly for Moral Re-Armament at Caux, Switzerland, and have seen it at work in many lands. Its challenge to a life of absolute moral standards has caused us much searching of heart and has made clear many places where it must be put to work in our country. We believe that this ideology is a key to the future of Japan and to a new era of comradeship between Occident and Orient in the task of remaking the world.'

The immediate effects of their mission were clear to see – their new-found unity, above party, class and point of view; their broader perspective on the world scene and Japan's place in it; their appreciation of America's generous policies toward Japan and her defence of South Korea; and their recognition of the priority of moral and spiritual recovery as a step toward political stability, economic recovery and the growth of a healthy democracy.

In their turn, the Japanese had rendered a significant service to others. They had presented a highly positive picture of a responsible leadership in post-war Japan; they had challenged many to re-evaluate their own priorities in private and public affairs; and they had made a small beginning in bridging the gulf of mistrust and hatred which many felt towards a recent enemy.

5

BIG STEP IN FAITH

On their return to Tokyo most members of the delegation were overwhelmed with the invitations to speak of their experiences and reports came back to us of the response as they addressed hundreds of audiences during the next few months. Representative Kitamura was received by the Emperor, who drew him out for two hours about the tour and asked some searching questions about MRA. All seven Diet Members were kept busy speaking individually and together. Their display of unity above party on many national issues soon caused a considerable stir. Nakasone spoke on the average three times a day and within three months of his return had addressed audiences of some 50,000. Kitamura embarked on a nation-wide lecture tour, as well as writing articles for many newspapers and magazines. Kuriyama was responsible for developing a strategy in the Diet to make MRA effective 'personally, in the home and in society'.

During the autumn these Members invited their colleagues in both Houses to a meeting in a Diet conference room to discuss 'the change which MRA brings in people's hearts, to remake society and the world.' The agenda covered: 'Teamwork to change society; What moved me to change; How my change changed my home; How to make MRA effective in the country.' There was no beating about the bush. Addressing the audience, in addition to the Diet Members, were a bank president, labour leader, president of a large manufacturing company, and managing director of the Japan Broadcasting Corporation.

Two of the most potent members of the returning delegation were Suzuki and Nakajima. Both spoke publicly and among their colleagues about the reconciliation between them at Caux, and of their changed philosophies. Suzuki called together the officers and men of the Osaka police force to tell them about his experiences and particularly about his new attitude towards protesters and trouble-makers. He said he had come to realize, through Nakajima's apology and honesty with him, that 'through the use of extreme measures in enforcing the law I stood out as a leader of the efforts to suppress workers and the labour movement.' He spoke of the hatred he had felt towards Communists and Koreans, whom he had considered as nothing but trouble-makers, and added that he had lost his hatred and found he could deal with members of the Communist Party and other militants as individual human beings.

Suzuki then called on the former chairman of the Prefectural Assembly; they had been political enemies for years, with a dozen lawsuits against each other. He apologized for his bitterness and asked for forgiveness. A few days later, at a public meeting, he repeated his apology and the other man apologized in return. Next day a newspaper headlined, 'Chief Suzuki Changes 180 Degrees.' During the next months he followed up his concern for his force of eight thousand policemen and their families. His men found they could talk with him about their domestic difficulties, as well as about police matters. A number of divided homes were reunited. Policemen on the beat wrote 'Absolute Honesty, Purity, Unselfishness and Love' on the walls of their patrol stations and tried to live by them. Their cordial attitude towards the public paid off: the soaring crime rate in the city dropped to the 1940 level.

Suzuki was bombarded with requests to speak to audiences beyond Osaka and aroused great interest among the leaders of the National Rural Police, the law enforcement agency which covered the whole country outside the large cities. He also spoke to officers of the Tokyo Metropolitan Police, the largest city police force in the world. His addresses and the friendships he developed marked the beginning of a closer accord between the police organizations in Japan which had often been at odds with each other since the end of the war.

Meantime Katsuji Nakajima was moving among the mountain villages of Nagano, where the Communists had their chief strength, and responded to many invitations to speak. In some of the 'red' villages he took his life in his hands. He was asked to serve on the prefectural mediation board and on several occasions in the next months was able to prevent industrial violence and civic disruption.

He also worked with Suzuki and Taizo Ishizaka, President of Toshiba, who had been with him at Caux, to demonstrate for labour and management a strategy of industrial teamwork.

Two other important areas of national life felt the impact of the returning delegation. The Governor of Telecommunications, a government corporation, was so impressed by what Kitamura told him that he arranged a series of talks to his senior staff, hoping to develop responsibility and co-operation among his 150,000 employees. The Governor of the National Railways, following restitution by one of his staff for dishonesty, gathered key personnel, together with leaders of the union, to hear about Moral Re-Armament. Both the telecommunications and railway unions were prime targets for Communist infiltration at that time.

These were encouraging results from the Mission, especially in making known to greater numbers the basic ideas to which those who had returned were committed. But those at the heart of the effort felt the need for a clearer strategy and a more unified programme. They returned the following summer to MRA's international conference, held that year on Mackinac Island, Michigan. The Sohmas and Mitsuis brought with them some of the former delegation – police chief Eiji Suzuki, Katsuji Nakajima, who had suffered in the Hiroshima bomb blast, and Chojiro Kuriyama, who headed a group of Diet Members in which the Socialists were strongly represented, including two dynamic women. There were also three government workers, each of whom held key jobs – the personnel chief of the National Railways, the chief training officer in the National Rural Police, and a member of the training staff of the Telecommunications Corporation. And the Toshiba Company sent its managing director and chairman of the union.

This was not as illustrious a delegation as that of the previous year, but its members had been wisely chosen. They would provide the leadership core for a programme of national rejuvenation; some of them were also positioned through their work to exert leverage on public policies.

Their experiences at Mackinac and afterwards on a journey through Washington and New York were similar to those of the earlier mission. For some of them, the decisions they made about their lives and work were more thorough-going, because Frank Buchman invited them to return to Mackinac from New York for a further week of meetings. For one of them, especially, it was a dramatic turning point.

Shidzue Kato was a prominent Socialist Member of the Upper House of the Diet. Born into a samurai family, she was first married to Baron Ishimoto and later to Kanju Kato, now a Member of the Lower House and a fiery Marxist labour leader who had spent time in prison for his crusading for workers' rights.

For some years Shidzue Kato had herself been an activist for social reforms, especially women's rights. At one of the meetings during this week she reached a crisis: in her words, 'I had come to America as a very proud woman, a Senator. As I sat and listened to what was being said in that room, it suddenly seemed as if I was at a funeral. I wept. It was the death of that pride of mine. But it was also the birth of a new woman, a humble woman. I had been known as a long-faced woman. My face changed, it became round and smiling.'

Her appearance changed so much, in fact, that when she flew back to Tokyo, her husband, peering through a window at the arrivals lobby at Haneda airport, did not at first recognize her. Another immediate result of her change was in her relationship with another member of the delegation, Mrs Satoko Togano, a Socialist Member of the Lower House. Although these two women belonged to the same party they had often been divided by jealousies and found themselves frequently on opposite sides of the rivalries which divided their party. From now onwards they became close friends and fellow fighters in their campaigns for social reforms. Their unity was to play an important part in uniting their party at times of stress.

Besides the Japanese, there were at Mackinac representatives of many Asian nations as well as Australia and New Zealand. Before they returned home Buchman planned a tour through West Coast cities during which they spoke at public meetings and receptions. The programme concluded with a conference, open to the public, in Los Angeles. The purpose of these events was to provide a platform from which the spokesmen from these countries could proclaim a new policy in the Pacific. Its keystone was peace and unity through a change in the motives of men and nations.

In July, 1951, that policy in the Pacific seemed a distant dream to most people. The Korean War was still being fought; the first of many meetings between United Nations and North Korean army officers had produced only deadlock; Communist guerrilla activity was increasing, from Indo-China to Indonesia; India, Burma, Vietnam, Malaysia and Indonesia were all plagued by violent conflicts between racial, religious and ideological factions. Faced by the threat of further outbreaks of war, Australia and New Zealand and the United States were planning a mutual military pact. In this setting any evidence of a uniting force at work in the Pacific was welcome news.

During these activities there was a development which made the conference all the more topical. The framers of a peace treaty with Japan completed their preparatory work and announced that a treaty-signing conference would be held in early September in San Francisco. The United States had persuaded most of her World War II allies that the time was now ripe to end the state of hostilities, bring the Occupation to a conclusion and restore independence to Japan. Agreement was reached reluctantly by some governments, and the Soviet Union rejected the plan and walked out of the conference. Australia and New Zealand and some other former enemies expressed serious reservations about the future integrity of a free Japan. As a result, the delegates to the Peace Treaty Conference met in San Francisco in an atmosphere of tension, heightened by a policy of segregating the Japanese, except for the conduct of official business.

Frank Buchman had laid plans to introduce a different note into the proceedings. As the delegates began to arrive in the city he put some of his colleagues to work developing friendships with them. Sumi Mitsui and I called on members of the Japanese advance party, some of whom we already knew. We had met five of the six official delegates, including Prime Minister Yoshida and Ichimada, Governor of the Bank of Japan. We also found we had a number of friends among the alternate delegates, advisers and press corps – Tetsu Katayama, Senator Setsuo Yamada, Fujimoto of *Mainichi* and others. Diet Members Shidzue Kato and Satoko Togano were also among the official observers.

As the conference opened, Buchman brought into San Francisco a larger group, including the cast of a musical play, *Jotham Valley* – MRA used the stage extensively to bring home its message. Each evening at the Geary Theatre scores of delegates were exposed to the magic of the play, which dramatized reconciliation in a Western ranching community. Among them were thirty Diet Members, who were deeply divided about the Peace Treaty. The Left wing of the Socialists was firmly opposed to it on the grounds that it moved Japan a step further in subordination to the United States, economically and in defence. The Socialist Party was fractured on the issue, and at the meal table and in the theatre our Socialist friends, Kato, Togano, Yamada and Katayama, were able to heal some of the divisions and establish a more positive perspective on the Treaty within the Party.

Each day, Frank Buchman hosted meals at a large round table in the restaurant at the top of the Mark Hopkins Hotel with a spectacular view of the city. His guests were delegates from the United States, France, Vietnam, Ceylon and other countries – and from Japan. All seemed appreciative of this opportunity to develop human ties with former enemies.

By the time the Treaty was formally signed on September 8 a better climate of understanding had been created between many of the individual delegates through the quiet work of Frank Buchman and a force of some 300 people permeating the national groups. The achievement was summed up by Robert Schuman, France's Foreign Minister, when he turned to Buchman on the final day of the conference and said, 'You made peace with the Japanese two years before we statesmen had the courage to sign it today.'

Before our Japanese friends returned home, several of them talked with me about the next steps in their strategy. They looked forward to their country's independence, which was to be granted next spring, but they were also concerned about the prospect of political and social disorder once the security of the US military was withdrawn. They felt an urgency to make their convictions more widely accepted and to build a nation-wide force of people capable of creating teamwork in industry, in political life and in society. They now had a small nucleus, including the Mitsuis and Sohmas, who were devoting their full time to the programme.

This was the moment, they urged, for me to join them, along with Jean and the children, to help them direct their efforts most effectively. Yukika Sohma and Shidzue Kato were the most pressing. They proposed that they and their friends should start looking for a suitable home for us which would also serve as a centre for their work.

Transplanting a family with a daughter four years old and a son of two was not a matter to be undertaken lightly. Living conditions were still spartan and the country's future uncertain. It would be a big step in faith, both for the Japanese and our family. Jean and I talked, thought and prayed about the invitation and then decided to launch out wholeheartedly. We invited two friends to accompany us. Mas Mitani was a Japanese American, born in Japan, and fluent in both languages. Tom Gillespie, a shipyard worker from the Scottish Clydeside, had been in the States for some years and we had worked closely together. His contacts had been especially with trade unionists in Europe and America.

They sailed with our family, along with Sumi and Hideko Mitsui, on the SS *President Cleveland* out of San Francisco in early November. For the Mitsuis it was a sad voyage. Their son Yori had died in Los Angeles after a long and painful spell of tuberculosis. His death was merciful, but a crushing blow to Sumi and Hideko. But before our ship reached Yokohama their faith had triumphed and they told us they would be marching shoulder to shoulder with us as we plunged into a new adventure.

6

SECURING A BASE

Among the crowd on the Yokohama dock as our ship drew in were two prominent groups. Our friends were beaming and waving, and nearby were people singing and holding a great red flag. They were members of the Communist Party, who had come to cheer a group of fifty Chinese students on our ship who were being deported from the United States to the Chinese mainland via Hong Kong.

The drive from Yokohama to Tokyo was not the best introduction to a beautiful country, but it was symbolic of the state of Japan. The road ran through a dismal jungle of industrial plants, vital to the economic welfare of Japan, but not pleasing to the eye. The area had been totally devastated during the war, but was now largely rebuilt in a makeshift manner. The scene was neither Orient nor Occident, modern nor ancient. We met oxcarts and Cadillacs, bicycle-rickshaws and army tanks, a super-highway and winding lanes so narrow you wondered if the car would go through. Threadbare poverty stood next to impressive modern architecture in the city.

On the drive we learned that our Japanese friends had not yet found a place to serve as a home for our family and the centre for our work. The Occupation had commandeered all suitable Western-style accommodation at the end of the war, and now the Korean War had increased even further the number of military and civilian personnel. The Sohmas had recently located a handsome house which they felt was what was needed. Its present owners, a Chinese couple, the Changs, wanted to sell. But first they had to find accommodation for themselves. A house they liked was on the market, but the owners could not yet move – a familiar 'musical chairs' situation in Tokyo.

Meantime, a generous friend from Washington, Margaret

Williams, then serving as a cultural attaché at the American Embassy in Tokyo, had invited our family to share her home. It was normally only available to married couples, but she was allowed to use the house because her work entailed a good deal of entertaining. The couple to whom it had been assigned were on a job in Washington. We settled in with gratitude. Tom Gillespie was invited to stay in the home of Taizo Ishizaka, President of Toshiba, and Mas Mitani was asked to the home of Niro Hoshijima, veteran Member of the Diet and one of the signatories of the San Francisco Peace Treaty.

Our first few days were spent with the nucleus who were giving their full time in order to sort out the priorities of the programme. We had been joined by an American, Rowland Harker, who had recently resigned a teaching post at a Japanese university. The Japanese represented a cross-section of society. The Mitsuis stood for business affluence in the mind of the public; the Sohmas for aristocracy and public service. They had been joined by Yasu's youngest brother, Toyotane, and his wife Tokiko. Toyo had resigned from his work as a medical doctor. Toneko Kimura was the daughter of a middle class banker. Katsuji Nakajima was the son of an employee of an impoverished samurai, himself apprenticed early in life as a worker in a metal factory. One of the young men working full time with us was Hideo Nakajima, no relative of Katsuji, from a poor farmer's home. As a naval cadet he was trained to operate a one-way manned torpedo. Fortunately for him the end of the war came before he was sent on his mission.

This was the team that worked, ate and spent a good deal of the day together. They were in many ways closer than most members of a family. In democratic America such a phenomenon is not common; in the Japan of the 1950's it was unique. The traditional divisions between old and young, rich and poor, senior and junior, were enough to prevent normal social relationships, let alone friendships, between classes. Even the language was designed to preserve the hierarchies. A man, for example, used a different word for 'I' when speaking to a man or a woman, superior or subordinate, young or old, acquaintance or stranger. It was small wonder that the cordial and candid life generated in this team made a considerable impression on those who encountered it.

As a result of the work of this nucleus and of the delegates to

Caux and Mackinac the past two summers, MRA was already becoming widely known, its concepts were being discussed in the news media, and there was a growing demand to learn more about its principles and how they could be applied in personal, business and public life. The general interest, together with the high regard in which MRA people were held, had led the government to amend its Public Safety Act to permit MRA meetings to be exempted from the provisions requiring all public gatherings to be specifically cleared by the authorities.

The full time team was being run ragged by the many demands for speakers, information and personal help from many parts of the country. A much larger force needed to be trained to be able to respond to these opportunities. Another priority was the development of the friendships already begun with that powerful group of politicians, businessmen, union officials, and professional people in whose hands rested the leadership of Japan. Just as important was to produce working models of co-operation in key segments of national life. The most immediate need was the securing of a base of operation.

There were no funds available for the purchase of the house which had been selected, so we needed to include senior men in the project. The one who had shown most interest in an MRA House was Hisato Ichimada, Governor of the Bank of Japan. He had sent a message on our arrival that he wanted to see me, and our first visit was to him. Sumi, Tom Gillespie and I found him bubbling with enthusiasm about his experiences in San Francisco at the Peace Treaty Conference. He said Buchman's efforts had been the one means of bridging the gulf between the Japanese and the other delegations, and he saw MRA as the ideal instrument for uniting Japan again with the family of free nations. During those days an idea had been born in his mind, to hold a Moral Re-Armament assembly in Japan as the first gesture after independence to open the doors of the country to the world, and especially to the neighbouring nations of Asia.

'But it will take more than a year,' he added, 'to build proper accommodation and roads, raise the funds, and make all the other preparations for entertaining overseas guests, as well as the Japanese delegates.' It sounded like planning for the Olympic Games. Ichimada went on to ask how matters stood regarding a centre for MRA. Sumi told him about the Chang house, and he said that if the place was adequate, we should press forward to get it. Since the Governor of the Bank of Japan was the key figure in any fund raising for the project, we heartily agreed, and Sumi asked for his help. He said he would give it, but others must step forward, as people too often left it to him to take the initiative.

During the next few days we had meals or conferences with a number of senior men, not merely about a centre, but about their concerns for the country. Among them were Chief Justice Kotaro Tanaka; Joji Hayashi, Speaker of the Lower House; Hisake Sato, Speaker of the Upper House; Amano, Minister of Education; Ichiro Ishikawa, President of the Federation of Economic Organizations; Taizo Ishizaka, who was not only President of Toshiba, but also of the Heavy Electric Manufacturers Association; Chikao Honda, publisher of *Mainichi*, the largest newspaper; and Tetsuo Furugaki, President of NHK, the Japanese public broadcasting corporation. We also saw the heads of the three biggest banks.

Our time with Honda of *Mainichi* was particularly enlightening. A shrewd observer of human frailties, he gave us some candid comments on people who had been at Caux and Mackinac. He described those who he felt meant business and those who did not. He said that Ichimada and Ishikawa had been trying to enlist his support for MRA through newspaper publicity and promoting fund raising. The journalists, and especially the magazine writers, he said, were mostly Marxists who were also cynics about human nature, and we would have our work cut out to gain their understanding and support. For his part, he would press forward with publication of the collected speeches of Frank Buchman, which Yukika Sohma had translated. The book, *Remaking the World*, was listed for early printing by *Mainichi*.

From two men in organized labour we also got a taste of battles ahead. Agune, Chairman of the Mitsui mineworkers union, came for an hour's visit. He had spoken 42 times about his recent experiences at the Mackinac conference and had found a good response among his 20,000 miners. But he said they were being exposed to a bitter campaign of class warfare, to which he felt that MRA was the only practical answer. We also had a long conversation with Takeo Muto, Chairman of Sohyo, the General Council of Trade Unions, most powerful of the labour organizations. He spoke frankly about the delicate balance of power in the unions between the Marxists and non-Marxists, and added that Moral Re-Armament was being smeared by the extreme Leftists as a 'tool of the capitalists.'

Then occurred an event which unexpectedly helped forward our pursuit of an MRA House. Senator and Mrs Alexander Smith and Senator Sparkman of Alabama, Smith's counterpart in the Democratic Party on the Senate Foreign Relations Committee, flew to Tokyo to join Foster Dulles, Special Adviser to the President, for an inspection tour of Korea. Margaret Williams, Jean and I invited them for dinner in her home to meet a cross-section of Japan's leadership to talk over some of the basic issues raised by the Peace Treaty and Security Pact. We invited Ichimada, Honda, Shidzue and Kanju Kato, Mrs Togano, Kuriyama and Hitoshi Kubo, National Chairman of the Telecommunications Workers Union, and also Horinouchi, Sumi and Hideko Mitsui, and Yasu and Yukika Sohma. We were taking a risk in inviting such a mixed company. The Socialists took a dim view of some parts of the Peace Treaty and officially opposed the Security Pact; Ichimada, Honda and Kuriyama were among the leading supporters of the government's policies towards the United States.

The evening began in an atmosphere of caution. Ichimada had to cut short a meeting with the Prime Minister and arrived looking exhausted; Kubo came directly from sit-down strike negotiations; Honda had had to change his plans and hurry up from Osaka. The Senators had never met any Japanese who were outspoken critics of American policy. Over a delicious turkey dinner the tension relaxed and we suggested to them that they ask their fellow guests their reactions to the treaty and pact. Their questions immediately produced a lively exchange between Honda, Ichimada, Kuriyama and Kanju Kato which served to highlight the basic differences of outlook between the conservatives and Socialists and between the businessmen and politicians. Yukika translated for Smith and Sparkman, who listened fascinated to the arguments. But even strong differences were dealt with harmoniously, and two significant points of agreement emerged from the discussions; the need for fundamental moral changes among the political parties, bankers, businessmen and labour unions; and the necessity for ideological training, both among the country's leaders and among the masses of the people.

As they left, Smith and Sparkman told us it had been a unique experience for them to listen to Japanese speaking with such frankness. We assured them that their presence had brought together elements of Japanese society which never normally met to discuss such important issues. To our surprise, our Japanese guests stayed on until midnight – we had found that usually guests took their leave by nine o'clock. They continued their discussion, seeming to enjoy their new and positive relationship.

An immediate result of the evening was a phone call from Ichimada's secretary to say that his boss had arranged a luncheon for December 25 in his official residence, to which he was inviting a select group of business leaders to consider support for MRA. He would like to have Sumi, Yasu, Tom and me join them. The evening had evidently stimulated Ichimada's imagination about how creatively an MRA House could be used. In Japan that date was just one more working day. We accepted happily, looking forward to it as a worthy celebration of Christmas.

To that meeting Ichimada invited Ishikawa, President of the Federation of Economic Organizations; Chigira, President of the second largest bank, Mitsubishi; Yamane, the top life insurance man in the country; and Inumaru, President of the Imperial Hotel. Ichimada started by asking Sumi to outline MRA's programme in Japan. Sumi did so and also spoke of the need for an adequate national fund and a home which could serve as the right centre for our work. Ichimada said he agreed that a house in Tokyo was the first priority. There was general agreement about the need for a centre, but also hesitancy to commit themselves until they had included a larger group. So they decided to hold a more representative gathering in a month's time to consider and act on the recommendations. When we compared notes afterwards, Sumi and Yasu were delighted, feeling that things were moving faster than they had expected. This was my first experience of the Japanese practice of seeking all viewpoints before working towards agreement.

Every few days I prodded Sumi to telephone Ichimada and the bankers to find out what they were planning. Sumi invariably hung up the phone to say that Ichimada's secretary had assured him that

'Mr Ichimada is thinking.' The phrase became a watchword among us, typifying the Japanese refusal to be hustled or to divulge any clue to their plans until they were good and ready. The Japanese people are activist, rather than contemplative, but they also go at their own pace and in their own way – something we Americans have a hard time grasping.

Then one morning word came from Ichimada that he would host his second meeting to discuss fund raising and an MRA House with 25 key men in business, the professions and politics. Among them were Ishizaka of Toshiba; Ishikawa; Chikara Kurata, President of Hitachi Electric; Shigeku Tashiro, President of Toyo Rayon; Yuasa, a leading manufacturer from Kyoto, and so on. He was also including from the Diet Kuriyama, Mrs Togano and Kanju Kato. Again Ichimada threw the ball to Sumi, who found himself chairing the meeting. The atmosphere was cool for a while, as Ichimada said nothing and the bankers and businessmen seemed to be waiting for him to give a lead. Sumi reported that the Changs were asking sixteen million yen for the house, and in those days, with the shortage of capital, that sum was considerable. It would have represented an investment of several million dollars in American terms.

Finally, Ichimada said that this amount could be raised in gifts and loans, and together they should undertake to do it. 'Fireball' Kato launched a powerful challenge, saying that he and many of his fellow Socialists would give as best they could out of their pockets. This seemed to shake up the businessmen, and Kurata said they should quit stalling and put up an interest free loan repaid as gifts were made. There was general agreement, the meeting ended, and Ichimada left the room. Sumi shot out after him and as they went down in the elevator, heard him say to one of the bankers, 'Do it. Arrange the loan.' 'Yes, sir,' said the banker.

During the closing days of March we obtained sufficient funds through gifts and interest free loans from the banks to make the full payment. The Changs promised to vacate the house on April 2, the day when their new home became free. On April 1, Margaret Williams received a cable from the couple in Washington in whose Tokyo home Margaret and we were living announcing that they were arriving next day. At first she thought it was an April Fool's joke. It was not. Our family moved out in the morning and the couple arrived in the afternoon – split second timing, and evidence to us that God honoured faith and prayer.

That afternoon Jean and I were entertained at a reception in the Diet by Members of several parties and both Houses. It was an informal meeting at which we and some of them spoke. Then we drove to the new house, located in an area where many of the embassies were grouped. The main house was a two-storied stone building, with a large room built on to the rear which could be used for meetings. A circular drive ran to an imposing covered porch entrance. A high wall surrounded the gardens which included a large lawn, stone lanterns, many flower beds, trees and ornamental rocks. There was a small cottage adjoining the garage where three could sleep.

Toyo and Tokiko Sohma moved in with our family and through their unselfish and devoted service ensured that the house was not merely a centre of activities but a warm-hearted and welcoming home. Others joined us as we put the cottage in shape and bought two more small houses adjoining the property. During the next six years hundreds of the famous and the humble, from every walk of life, passed through the doors of this gracious building. Luncheons and dinners, and breakfast too, were served for visitors, who came for many different reasons – to seek help for personal problems, to learn about what we were doing, to plan how to heal divisions and break deadlocks in family life, industrial affairs and national issues. Senior Diet Members of opposing parties would breakfast each week in its privacy to forge a strategy to deal constructively with national issues. We would entertain secretly at night an acting Prime Minister, who came to seek wisdom about a political crisis. And in this home, the only place on Japanese soil to which they would come, citizens from two former enemy countries met for the first time with Japanese.

The first event was a reception to which came a hundred friends from the Diet, industry, labour and government, along with their wives. As they mingled on the lawn outside the living room, Senator Setsuo Yamada of Hiroshima asked permission to speak. His theme was that this home was even more important for Japan than the American Embassy because here was born a spirit of harmony between representatives of different elements in the country – a unique service to post-war Japan. One of the guests was Hideo

Yamahana, National Chairman of the Chemical Workers and a prominent member of the Left-wing Socialist Party. A long-time associate of Kanju Kato, they had been in prison together in the early days as revolutionary Marxists. He arrived suspicious and critical, a champion of class war in surroundings which suggested affluence. During the afternoon he mellowed and when he bade us goodbye his large round face was lit by a warm smile. He would become a close colleague.

The men who undertook the purchase of the MRA House also made possible a start in the financing of its operations. The Ministry of Education registered MRA as a non-profit organization with a subsidiary association which supporting corporations could join. After considering the matter carefully and deciding to support the programme, a company included the item in its budget and then left us to use the money as we saw fit. On our part, we undertook training programmes and other activities which resulted in greater harmony and productivity and a spirit of creativity in many of these enterprises. Along with the companies, a growing number of individuals and families made regular contributions, many of them at considerable sacrifice from their small incomes. The basis on which we proceeded was the faith that if we did what was needed in society, our own needs would be met.

7

CREATING A FORCE

Securing a base of operations was secondary in importance to the task of developing men and women who would take on together the commitment to live and work for a new nation and a new world. Closest to the nucleus of full time workers were a few families, and especially three men who had been on the delegation to Mackinac the previous summer. Each of them had begun to apply their convictions in their own field of work and with their wives and children. Kozo Kimura, Yoshinobu Kataoka and Juzo Tsuruta each held key positions in strategic national organizations.

While Eiji Suzuki's fame was spreading in police circles, Kozo Kimura was becoming known to many in the National Rural Police, of which he was chief of the Patrol and Traffic Division, responsible for twelve thousand patrol stations throughout Japan. The NRP at that time stood in the front line of national security. Attacks by Communist militants on some of the isolated one-man posts had resulted in death and injury to police. Kozo had two major objectives: to train every policeman to win the confidence and respect of the people in their communities; and to overcome the local and regional jealousies and frictions among his force, so that the police across the country could work more efficiently together. This was of the greatest importance in dealing with crime, since American and Japanese fear of the resurgence of a police state had led to the fracturing of the police forces to the point of inefficiency. Kimura arranged for us to hold regular training sessions for senior staff of the NRP, as well as meetings for officers of the Tokyo Metropolitan Police. He told us later that these meetings increased his effectiveness in advancing his work.

His experience at Mackinac transformed Kataoka from a cautious bureaucrat to a creative innovator, startling his colleagues and intriguing his employees. Up to this time the National Railway

Workers Union, one of the strongest in the country, had been a source of violent turmoil. Kataoka's reconciliation with many of his colleagues, and his practical application of 'not who's right, but what's right' in his dealings with his staff made their impact on his fellow directors and on the union. From the end of 1951 many meetings were held at National Railways headquarters and at various railway stations around the country. In fact, during the next five years the National Railways became linked with Moral Re-Armament in the minds of thousands of Japanese. Hundreds of railwaymen, at all levels of the corporation, were active in its development in their areas. Directors, district managers, station masters and rank and file workers helped to create an atmosphere of trust and integrity.

The telephone and telegraph system in Japan was run by the government's Telecommunications Corporation, and its union was the target of a Communist strategy of disruption. When Tsuruta became a senior officer in the Training Department he went to work to improve relations between workers and management and to strengthen the hand of the sound elements in the union. Through him we came to know two successive national chairmen of the union, both of whom became our close allies. Later, Tsuruta worked with the Governor of Telecommunications to establish regular MRA training courses for thousands of their employees. Before long, Telecommunications became known as a model of industrial teamwork.

These and other men and women met with us frequently and our gatherings were seasoned with discussions about the right course to follow in home life and day-to-day living and in their professional responsibilities. To meet a public demand to know more about Moral Re-Armament, we accepted the offer of the National Railways to use their central hall for weekly meetings in downtown Tokyo. This meeting served several purposes – to make MRA better understood, assisted by good press coverage; to give experience to people in expressing their convictions; and to provide an occasion for them to enlist their friends in a programme of action.

Each of these public meetings was different, fascinating in the unexpected variety of those who had something new to say. At the first meeting, for example, the speakers included a group from the National Railways – a director, two station masters and a redcap

— a student from Tokyo University, a conservative Diet Member and the commander and a patrol man of the Imperial Guard of the Palace. The following week, among the spokesmen were a mechanic in an electric plant, a housewife, a Shinto priest, the head of the National Rural Police Training School, the managing director of a Kobe wharf company, the student body president of Osaka University, and the head of the Tokyo central telephone exchange.

While the speakers were varied, the underlying themes persisted: personal moral change; homes with a new honesty and happiness; plants and offices freed from tension, feuds and cheating; citizens in public and private life awakened to a new responsibility in society. Several hundred attended each week and people began coming from other areas. No hard line was drawn between those who were fully committed to living the life and those who wanted to have some part in the programme. As a result, great organizations such as the Rural Police, Telecommunications Corporation and National Railways later became to some degree extensions of the MRA team, carrying its basic ideas to thousands beyond our reach.

We were soon flooded with requests to hold meetings in various parts of the country and embarked on the road with small teams to Osaka, Kobe, Kyoto, Hiroshima and smaller towns. Everywhere these teams were interviewed by the press and radio and usually the mayor, governor or other dignitaries were on hand to welcome and entertain and sponsor the events. The Mackinac and Caux alumni were often the hosts and usually took an active part with the travelling team. A network of cells began to spring up across the country and we started publishing a bi-weekly information service for them as well as for the growing number of friends we were making in all areas of life. Its subscribers soon included a high percentage of the country's leaders and in our conversations with them we found that most of them read it with care.

Along with the National Railways, Rural Police and Telecommunications, another influential association became a participant in the national programme. The heavy electric manufacturing industry was a mushrooming element in Japan's economic recovery. It was beginning the greatest over-all growth in the domestic and overseas markets together of all Japanese industries. In 1950 television sets, refrigerators and washing machines were almost unknown in

77

Arnett Branch Library
310 Arnett Blvd.
Rochester, N. Y. 14619

Japanese homes. By the end of the decade seven out of ten homes had TV sets, and the average home had come to depend on its washer and refrigerator. During the same period the world began to become aware of Japanese transistor radios and most kinds of electronic equipment. Without this boom the country's economy could not have expanded as it did. The electrical industry's exports had a major role in obtaining the credit needed to purchase from abroad the bulk of Japan's raw materials, fuel and foodstuffs it had to import.

Shortly after we arrived in Tokyo we were invited to speak at a luncheon meeting of the Electrical Manufacturers Association at which the presidents and top management of the four largest companies were present – Hitachi, Toshiba, Mitsubishi and Fuji. They stayed for three hours, listening and asking many questions. It was in effect a training meeting in industrial teamwork, and the convictions of the speakers were carried to a much wider audience. An account of the meeting was published in the *Nikkeiren Times* – the periodical of the Japanese Employers' Association, read by most businessmen:

'The Heavy Electric Management Association had been aware of the importance of Moral Re-Armament ever since Mr Ishizaka, the President of Tokyo Shibaura Electric Company, attended the World Assembly at Caux two years ago, and Mr Takahashi, the managing director, and two labour leaders from the company attended the Mackinac Assembly last year. Then several international representatives of MRA arrived in Japan and the Association held several occasions to hear about MRA. As is generally known, post-war Japan has suffered economic and moral confusion, which has led our labour-management relationships down a wrong path. Sound elements in management and labour unions are making special efforts to rebuild their relationships. They have noted with great interest that the application of the MRA ideology to labour-management relations will affect the increase of production and of job security. . . .

'We have moved from an era where man's life is controlled by economic factors to an era where an idea or ideology can control our lives by utilizing economic factors. A big idea –

78

Communism – which vitally affects politics and industry today has brought a great loss to the world through division and strife.

'What can answer a vital ideology of either left or right, which might sway a nation? Moral Re-Armament is the answering ideology. . . .'

Following this luncheon, there were similar occasions with the top management and union leaders of two of the companies, Toshiba and Mitsubishi. The company presidents were present and the heads of the executive committees of the unions took part. Each gathering, in company time, lasted for more than three hours, as a panel of eight spoke and answered questions. The most significant feature of these events was that for the first time management and labour of large companies sat down together for any purpose other than to negotiate their differences. They marked the beginnings of teamwork in an industry notorious for its violent confrontations.

Sumi Mitsui architected another important business gathering during that first month. He arranged a luncheon to meet the heads of the twenty-six Mitsui companies. These large corporations had formed the huge Mitsui empire which was broken up by the Americans at the end of the war. In reality, however, the heads of the companies worked quietly to renew their close association, even though legally separate, and by the early 1950's had already started to exert a powerful influence on the economic life of the country.

Daiichi Bussan, the trading company, Mitsui Bank, Mitsui Chemical, Mitsui Mining, Japan Steel Works, Mitsui Shipbuilding, Toyo Rayon, and so on, spanned a great variety of economic activities. Their senior executives, although at times in disagreement and with conflicting interests, nevertheless were members of a team who were able to pool a great amount of vital information which enabled them to forecast market trends and tailor production and distribution most effectively.

This luncheon lasted for three hours and gave us an opportunity to paint for these men a broad picture of the world and the evidence of a positive force at work to heal divisions and answer problems. Several of them became close allies.

Perhaps the most significant development in team building was through almost daily contact with prime movers of the country, –

men and women in the Government, Diet, business, finance and industry, labour unions and the professions – who directed the course of affairs.

In some respects the development of teamwork among Japanese leaders was easier and in other ways more difficult than in other countries. A positive factor was that in Japan, unlike some countries, there was no one outstanding figure – a Roosevelt, Churchill, De Gaulle or Adenauer. Instead, the achievements of the men who led the country's resurgence were largely the result of their ability to work closely together, rather than of their individual brilliance. On the other hand, there was normally little common ground between the protagonists of conflicting ideas – conservatives and socialists, labour and management, large and small businesses, intellectuals and activists, urban and rural life.

Before long, certain ones began to stand out as reliable friends and allies who could be counted on to devote time and thought, beyond their immediate responsibilities, to what needed to be done in the country and have a hand in doing it together. It was usually the busiest men and women who responded the most. In the Diet, Kitamura and Kuriyama, the two Toganos and Katos, Hoshijima, Shinkichi Ukeda (a Socialist) and Setsuo Yamada were the nucleus around whom a growing number from both Houses became spokesmen for moral principles and began to apply them to their work. They represented several factions in the government coalition of conservative parties, and the moderate elements in the Socialist Party. A couple of years later a dynamic group of young Left-wing Socialists in the Upper House began working with them – Kubo, Yamahana, Suzuki and Nagaoka, men who had each headed national labour unions.

Among those in the business field who played a prominent part were some of the most senior leadership – Ichimada and Ishizaka; Ishikawa, President of the Federation of Economic Organizations; Hayakawa, President of Nippon Express, largest freight haulers; Tadao Watanabe, President of Sanwa, the largest bank; Seiiji Iino, head of the Iino Shipping Lines; Konichi Moroi, President of the National Employers Association; and Michisuke Sugi, President of the Osaka Chamber of Commerce. Among officials in public life were Hamai, Mayor of Hiroshima; Haraguchi, Mayor of Kobe; Akama, Governor of Osaka; Amano, Minister of Education; and

MRA House in Tokyo

Mrs Shiro Ohashi (left), President
of the Japan Women's University,
with Mrs Hide Inouye, President,
Women's Social Educational
Association of Japan

Max Bladeck, Chairman, Works Council, Rheinpreussen Pit, Moers

A thousand policemen fought with 20,000 demonstrators in the streets of Tokyo, May 1952

Kajii, Governor of Telecommunications Corporation. In other fields were Honda, and the President of Japan Women's University, Mrs Ohashi.

Those who undertook the work of mobilizing the best in the country and trying to change what was wrong found their horizons expanding beyond their familiar spheres. Businessmen began getting to know union men as people, conservatives and socialists stepped out of their normal confrontation roles with each other. Bureaucrats started associating with people who had been only statistics. Lasting personal friendships developed above party, class and point of view, where few had existed before.

This bridge-building function among the country's leaders was apparent at one of the first formal luncheons we gave at the MRA House. The guest of honour was Parks Shipley, a New York banker closely associated with MRA. Around the table sat Ichimada and Keizo Shibusawa, bankers; Niro Hoshijima, senior conservative Diet Member; two big employers, Shinichi Hayakawa of *Nippon Express* and Shigeki Tashiro of Toyo Rayon; old-time Marxist Kanju Kato and Shidzue Kato, and Hideo Yamahana and Setsuo Yamada, respectively Left- and Right-wing Socialists. At the end of the luncheon, Kanju Kato, who had often flayed 'Wall Street imperialism' in his speeches, said he agreed with the American banker that MRA was the only adequate answer to the hostility of extreme Left and Right. Hoshijima remarked on how revolutionary it was for Ichimada and Kato to be enjoying the same company. Not so, said Ichimada – that was normal in Moral Re-Armament. Ichimada added that MRA was the only hope for Japan and he put it to the American to fight that it become the policy of his government. Senator Yamada challenged all present to constitute themselves an informal committee to head the financing of MRA in Japan. The Katos offered a beautiful gold screen from their home for the House, and Ichimada and Hayakawa followed suit by offering paintings.

Such a gathering anywhere else in Tokyo in the early 1950's would have been hard to find. From the start we learned that the best way to bridge the social, political and economic chasms was to create situations, such as this luncheon, in which former enemies could fight shoulder to shoulder for a common goal. And this was especially important in a land which still bore many of the marks of a feudal society.

Toyo Sohma unconsciously provided two examples soon after our arrival. A few days after he had told me that few Japanese any longer stood in awe of the Emperor he came racing into the living room at MRA House to tell Jean that Princess Chichibu, sister-in-law of the Emperor, had arrived unannounced at the front door. Pale-faced, he called in agitation, 'Come quickly! What should we do with her?' Later, he was driving me through the city and made an illegal turn. A young policeman stopped us and asked to see Toyo's driving licence. He studied it and then asked if Toyo was from the family in the town of his birth. Toyo said he was indeed. 'Ah, Mr Sohma,' said the policeman, bowing deeply, 'My father served your family. Please excuse me for having stopped you, and please, sir, be careful to observe the traffic regulations.' He then returned the licence and bowed us on our way.

Anyone who became acquainted with MRA could not help notice the variety of people who rubbed shoulders amiably and with mutual respect – the laundryman, who was freed from alcoholism, was soon as much at home in MRA House as the Chief Justice of the Supreme Court. A country girl from an impoverished family had a valued place there, just as did a lady-in-waiting to the Empress. Differences and distinctions remained, but a commitment to personal change created bonds of mutual confidence and loyalty from which grew a uniting national force.

8

ANSWERING CLASS WAR

The spring of 1952 was a testing time for Japan. On April 28 the Peace Treaty was to come into effect, with the Occupation ending and the country regaining its independence. The day was awaited eagerly, but with some apprehension, especially by Yoshida's government. The Security Treaty with the United States and some of her Pacific allies would also come into effect. The pact bound Japan to America, on whom she must rely for military security and for whom she would continue to provide bases and facilities for a considerable military force. Powerful elements in Japanese society were strongly opposed to these ties with the West – the Communists, Left-wing Socialists, many intellectuals and leaders of most of the labour unions, and also those businessmen who resented economic dependence on the United States, which had closed the markets of mainland China and the Soviet Union.

The militant Left was small in numbers and its activities were restricted by law, but its propaganda against the Government's foreign and domestic policies was powerful. Its shrewdly conceived offensives for 'peace' and against 'American Imperialism,' together with its demands for higher wages for the workers, fell on receptive ears, especially among labour leaders and intellectuals. The propaganda was all the more effective at this time because the Peace Treaty spelled the end of some sheltering conditions of the Occupation. Countries such as South Korea and the Philippines and Indonesia were demanding a full measure of reparations for the war; some raw materials would no longer be obtainable at favourable prices. There was a serious lack of capital; growing inflation and recurrent industrial unrest due to relatively low wages were mounting. Taxes were high and going higher, with a substantial item for national defence appearing in the budget for the first time. And many feared that the boom produced by the Korean war, through the US military's need for Japanese supplies and services, would soon collapse.

We were very much aware of these explosive elements in the country and had been trying to take some steps with the leaders of the Socialist parties and the key labour unions. Tom Gillespie and Mas Mitani spent two hours with Minoru Takano, Secretary-general of Sohyo, the General Council of Trade Unions, the largest and most powerful of the labour organizations, with a membership of four million. They also met with Takeo Muto, its Chairman, and a number of the staff. As a result of the time with these men and with some of the Socialist Diet Members, Gillespie was invited to speak at the national conference of the Left-wing Socialists. Some four hundred of them heard him propose that the surest way to lasting changes in society was through changing the attitudes of people. Shidzue Kato then invited him to speak at the Right-wing Socialist conference, at which she was in the chair. Gillespie was the only foreigner to be present at both conferences and the first to speak at them for some years. Although there were members of the Communist Party in the Left-wing audience, he was well received on both occasions.

May Day, celebrated by organized labour around the world, was to be observed in Japan by parades of workers in every city. In Tokyo, Sohyo planned a march through the centre of the city to Hibiya Park. The unions were joined by the two Socialist Parties, several thousand university students, as well as farmers, women's organizations and a hard core of Communists who skilfully forged these diverse elements into a united demonstration. The marchers carried banners with slogans denouncing the Government's anti-subversive measures, national defence policies and alliance with the United States. Speakers were to address the crowd of some half-million when they arrived in Hibiya Park and then the marchers were to disperse. But they did not.

Many carried banners on poles. They stripped off the flags to reveal steel-tipped spears. Government intelligence had warned of preparations for rioting, and the Metropolitan Police had been reinforced by ten thousand National Police Reserve, the only semi-military organization which Japan then possessed.

Early that afternoon I was driving downtown for a conference with officials at the Ministry of Finance. As I swung down a boulevard leading to the Imperial Palace grounds on one side and Hibiya Park on the other, I came on a tumultuous scene. The major crossroad was swarming with people, running, pushing, shouting and fighting. As I arrived at the intersection, it was blocked by a stream of milling people. With the most helpless feeling I sat and watched bands of fierce looking men wielding spears and staves, locked in combat with blue-helmeted police fighting back with truncheons. Further down the boulevard, black smoke was rising from automobiles which had been overturned and set on fire. To my left, on the towering stone walls of the Palace grounds, rising from the moat, there were more struggling, yelling crowds. Around my car surged hundreds of men and women, pushed this way and that by the tides of fighting and caught up in the excitement of the scene.

I had never before been in the middle of a riot and found the raw emotions of the crowd almost overwhelming, a physical battering of the senses. I had rolled up the windows and some older people, with fear in their eyes, began knocking on the glass. I could not understand what they were saying, but by their gestures they were clearly urging me to get out and run. I was on the point of doing so when a gap opened up between the knots of combatants and spectators in front of me. Feeling no doubt as did Moses, with Pharaoh's forces on his heels when the Red Sea parted before him, I shoved the Chevy into gear and leaped forward across the intersection. I raced past damaged burnt cars with licence tags showing they were owned by military or civilian Americans. The pungent fumes of burning rubber were thick in the air.

Later, the Attorney General announced the casualties of the day's violence – two killed and 200 injured among the rioters; twelve foreigners attacked and 76 policemen injured. Rioting on a lesser scale took place in many cities and the whole country was shocked by the outbreaks. Most Japanese deplored the violence, even though many of them approved the goals of the Socialist and labour unions. The effect of the May Day events was to turn the majority against the Communists and the extreme Left. And Yoshida's government pushed hard for more severe limits on their activities. But we were in close touch with leaders of the unions and the Socialists and understood that the far Left had effective influence on Japan's economic and political life through its infiltration of Sohyo and the

Socialists and through its ability to exploit popular causes. We talked together about the urgent need to unite and inspire our friends on many fronts if Japan was to develop as a free and prosperous country.

A main focus of our work in April and May 1952 was the selection of a delegation to the World Assembly which was to open that year at Mackinac in late May. The forming of a delegation to Mackinac and Caux became an annual task each spring and proved to be an essential element in developing men and women of calibre for the moral and spiritual re-armament of their country. An overseas trip was no longer the novelty for senior Japanese which it had been a couple of years earlier. Many leaders in government and business were now able to attend international conferences, so we were no longer overwhelmed by requests from top-ranked men and women. But there were still plenty of applicants, and our concern was to select those on whom we could count for responsibility in developing a national programme.

The biggest problem was the same as we had encountered in 1950, currency exchange, and it was one which would continue to dog us. The government hoarded hard-won dollars in order to pay for foreign raw materials and priority items, so the dollar exchange available for foreign travel was strictly limited and was allocated primarily for those going on important business trips. Hoshijima talked to Ikeda, Minister of Finance, and paved the way for visits to officials in his Ministry. Our argument was that our conferences at Mackinac and Caux provided ideal opportunities for Japanese to break through the barriers which still prevented Japan from reaching her world markets. The Government started by allowing funds for only six to travel, and although they eased this a little, we had to ask MRA in America for help in paying for the expenses of others. We collected from those travellers who could afford it payment in yen to cover the cost of their trip.

At the end of May a delegation of twenty left for Mackinac including seven Diet Members, two labour leaders, a surgeon, the Deputy Mayor of Kobe and the president of the student body of Osaka University. There was one other member of the group who was a national figure. Keizo Shibusawa had been Minister of Finance and Governor of the Bank of Japan. He was a prominent member of the Government party and one of the most influential men in the country. He was also the grandson of Viscount Shibu-sawa, who had been a host to Frank Buchman many years earlier. The Diet Members demonstrated an impressive super-party team-work, since they included Kanju Kato and Yamahana on the Left-wing of the Socialists, and two convinced conservatives, Isao Matsudaira, a charming member of the former aristocracy, and now owner of a steel plant; and Saichi Yamada, a textile manufac-turer. Matsudaira told the conference audience he had come to realize that the May Day riots and other violence were the results in part of the indifference of his class to the needs of people, and also the result of the cynicism of youth towards politicians. It was his responsibility, he said, to regain their trust.

Yamahana talked about the urgent need to create a working unity in the country and said that the personal trust among poli-ticians of differing convictions, such as was being developed at Mackinac, must be multiplied in the Diet. Kanju Kato, the veteran ideologist, said that in MRA's principles lay the only answer to Communism and revolution. Working together on the basis of 'what's right, not who's right,' he said, we could win the confidence of the ordinary man.

At the end of the assembly the Japanese set off on a familiar itinerary – Detroit, Washington, New York, Chicago, and the West Coast. The Diet Members had two conferences at the State Department, during which they answered questions very frankly, giving a realistic picture of the divisions in Japan and startling the Americans by their demonstration of teamwork and the clarity of their convictions. Vice-President Barkley gave a reception; they were entertained at a luncheon in the Senate and on the following day were lunch guests of Senators Wiley, Sparkman and Smith.

After a full schedule in Los Angeles they reached San Francisco, the last stop. By now the Diet Members were becoming impressive spokesmen and the symbol of a new-found unity. Their growth was not achieved without some lively encounters. The most memorable occurred during a visit to the San Francisco City Hall. The Mayor at that time was a smooth-talking politician who had agreed to receive the group, but when they entered his office he was off-hand in his greeting and soon made it clear that he wanted to move on to other business. The Diet Members took their visits to American officials very seriously. They liked to ask searching questions about political, social and economic matters. They took notes of the answers and were well prepared with information about conditions in Japan.

After a few minutes of platitudes, the Mayor ended the visit. I was walking down the broad marble staircase under the great dome of the building when angry shouts burst out behind me, echoing around in the stately lobby. I turned around to see Kanju Kato, red in the face, waving his arms and letting it be known to the world that he had not come across the Pacific to be treated like a stupid child by a stuffed shirt American mayor. It was clear at that moment how he had earned his nickname, 'Fireball'.

By the next day, Kanju had recovered and when the delegation left for Tokyo three days later, he issued a statement to the press on behalf of the whole group:

'At present the world is in conflict and turmoil. We face the choice of dictatorship and democracy, slavery and freedom, war and peace. The lessons of Korea teach us that force alone does not bring victory over the strategy of Communist violence. Victory can only be obtained by a superior ideology and a superior statesmanship. . . . Our delegation represents opposite poles of Japanese politics, industry and labour. In spite of this varied representation we are united in our determination to put this answer to work in Japan and make her a lighthouse for Asia.'

On their return, Kanju and Yamahana with Shidzue – three of the most prominent among the Socialists – and Matsudaira and Saichi Yamada, staunch conservatives, spoke to a large and representative audience at the Industry Club. Their appearance together in public and their obvious harmony caused widespread interest. A General Election was to be held early in October and bitter fighting was going on, not only between the parties, but within them, especially among the conservatives.

The Liberal Party, largest in the Government coalition, was divided by a serious struggle for power by two of its members. Prime Minister Yoshida's position was assailed by Ichiro Hatoyama, who had been head of the party until he was purged by the Occupation authorities. His political exile now over, as leader of a powerful faction, he was challenging Yoshida for the premiership. The Socialists were hoping to make big gains out of the conservative split. Hoshijima, now one of the most respected members of the Liberal Party, went to work on the two men, both of whom he knew well. They were reconciled for the time being, and Hatoyama withdrew his challenge to the top post. Hoshijima told us that he had been able to help stop the feuding because of what he had learned through Moral Re-Armament.

The following summer, in 1953, MRA's annual assembly was held in Caux, Switzerland, with the emphasis on teamwork in industry. This theme fitted well with our conviction that we should give priority to men in charge of management-labour relations in the big companies where we were at work. More than anything we now needed to produce demonstrations of an answer to class war, which still dominated much of Japan's industrial scene. By the time the delegation left in early August it included the top negotiators for management in the National Railways, Toshiba Electric, and Onoda Cement, the vice-presidents of two steel companies, and the union heads of Toshiba and Hitachi Electric.

Asian countries were represented in greater numbers than ever before, and the Japanese found themselves face to face with people who had suffered at the hands of their military in World War II – among them, the Speaker of the Malayan Parliament, an Australian Member of Parliament and a British labour union official. To the amazement of the Japanese these individuals apologized for their hatred, from which they had been freed. In this healing atmosphere most of the delegation made decisions affecting their personal and family living as well as their work. Saburo Nakahata, of the National Railways, and Tago and Toshio Nishiumi, the steel men, and those from the electric companies, all made such decisions and these were to have their impact on their companies.

The Japanese distinguished themselves in visits with Congressmen and government officials on the way home through Washington. The highlight of their time there, however, was a visit in the home of John Riffe, a veteran labour leader, now an invalid, with not long to live. John told them in simplest terms about the change in his life – his honesty with his wife Rose and their children; his reconciliation with industrialists with whom he had been at war; his role in bringing together the feuding heads of the CIO and AFL into one united organization. He said the key had been the daily illumination and direction he had received in quiet times before God, seeking His way through all the tangled paths of organized labour and industrial strife. Riffe asked them about unions in Japan and they gave him an honest picture, stressing the efforts of the Communists to disrupt relations. John said they were fighting the most important battle in the world, to create hate-free, greed-free, fear-free men and nations.

9

PARTNERS IN PRODUCTIVITY

The men who returned in the 1953 Caux delegation proved to be the nucleus of a force which fought to replace labour-management class-war antagonism with a philosophy of industrial teamwork. The day after their arrival in Tokyo, the delegates were given the opportunity to speak at a public meeting in the Industry Club. Taizo Ishizaka, President of Toshiba, introduced them before a distinguished audience of business executives, union officials and Diet Members.

The last two speakers, Ryozaburo Kawahara, Toshiba's industrial chief, and Etsuro Yamamura, head of the union, received the greatest applause. Everyone present was aware of the grim history of the company and the union. Yamamura closed by saying he had often demanded fair distribution of the company's profits, but had only given his wife and children one-third of his wage packet. From now on he was going to fight for workers' rights on the basis of what was right and pledged to conduct the current wage dispute in the spirit of MRA.

Because of the earlier Communist control of the Toshiba workers there was still no formal contract between company and union, and wages and other matters had to be renegotiated twice a year. Talks had been dragging on with little progress and the union had set a date for a strike if no settlement had been reached before then. Kawahara and Yamamura immediately plunged into action. They were an unlikely team. Kawahara was a quiet, dapper, self-contained man who might have been mistaken for a government bureaucrat. Yamamura was a brawny, big-chested fellow, with a ready laugh, a flamboyant manner and an enormous waxed moustache. During their trip abroad they had talked over honestly a number of the differences between them. They apologized to each other for their hostile attitudes and had become firm friends.

As soon as they entered the negotiations the atmosphere changed. The sessions became shorter, with each side simply stating its proposals and listening to those of the other side, instead of indulging in long-winded wrangling. The union made no more unreasonable demands, but had solid facts to support each request. On the day before the strike deadline, Kawahara announced that the company had agreed to most of the demands and had honestly gone as far as it could go – any further concessions would be detrimental to everyone. The union representatives responded that if Kawahara said that was true, they believed him and the union would accept the offer. The union executive approved the decision by a vote of 22 to 12.

A few months later, Hasegawa, former chairman of the Toshiba union, told us that the new co-operation between management and union had had very practical results. One plant had been running eight million yen in the red each month and the company had decided to close it. But within a few weeks after Kawahara and Yamamura returned from Caux the plant was operating three million yen in the black, and the company reversed its decision.

The positive impact of improvements in Toshiba was soon felt by the five other major heavy electrical manufacturers. At an informal industrial conference to which management and labour from all these companies came, they heard Toshiba representatives talk in detail of what they had accomplished. This was followed by meetings in other factories in the heavy electric and other industries, at which Kawahara and Yamamura and their colleagues spoke of their new relationship and its practical results. It was not long before similar teamwork began to develop in Mitsubishi, Fuji, Hitachi and other electrical manufacturing plants.

This harmony could not have come at a more decisive moment for the whole industry. A few months earlier I had visited Ishizaka in his Toshiba office. During our conversation he had reached across his desk and handed me a small amber plastic object. 'This little thing is going to revolutionize our company and all of Japanese business,' he said. I knew nothing about electronics and must have looked sceptical. But Ishizaka's words were prophetic. He had returned from visiting General Electric, their affiliate in the States, and brought back this silicon chip, a forerunner of a stream of patents received by Toshiba and the electric manufacturers, as well as others developed by themselves.

An era of bitter conflict began to give way to one of creative human partnership just at the time when these technological advances opened the road to a huge world and domestic market for this industry. Without the basis of such teamwork it is a question whether the electrical manufacturers could have risen to the opportunity as they did. As it was, the good results in these companies spilled over into other key industries in whose hands the 'economic miracle' took shape. Synthetic textiles, shipbuilding and steel all benefited from MRA men at work in their plants, their management associations and their unions. Toyo Rayon, the leading synthetic textile manufacturer, and later Yawata Steel and Ishikawajima Shipbuilding were among those concerns which soon could cite examples of stoppages prevented, working conditions improved, pay raises and rising productivity.

The man primarily responsible for a transformation in management-labour relations at the big Ishikawajima Shipyards was the young president of the union, Renzo Yanagisawa. His personal life was turned around and his family united – his wife no longer a 'union widow'. Renzo took a fresh look at his responsibilities and his way of conducting union business and brought a breath of fresh air into the wage negotiations there after they had dragged on while he was abroad at Caux. He persuaded his executive that they should put all their cards on the table with management – their analysis of company costs and profits and their own honest objectives in wage demands and fringe benefits. They did so, and at the same time challenged management to open its books to the union. Such an idea was unheard of at that time. The company president, Toshiwo Doko, with whom we had had some lively sessions in recent months, was a man of vision and wide perspectives who was later to follow in Ishizaka's shoes as the top business leader in Japan. Doko surprised his colleagues and the union by accepting Yanagisawa's challenge; a move which placed labour relations on a firmer footing in the company and made them a model for other industries. It was not long before a new spirit was entering the Mitsui and Hitachi shipyards, when the shipbuilding industry was gearing up for enormous expansion, to make Japan the world's leading producer of ships.

Other members of the Caux delegation were also applying what they had learned on their tour. Ishigaki, chairman of the 12,000 member union at Hitachi Electric, spoke to his whole union about the changes in his life. He told them he had stopped wasting a large part of his pay on gambling, *sake* and tobacco; his home was now happy. He apologized to them for his lack of self-discipline as their representative. The union members voted to make regular contributions to MRA and afterwards the head of his department came to him to get his help in straightening out his life. Another delegation member, Nishiumi, who owned an engineering company, got his employees together to tell them about Caux and made several innovations in his company, including a more generous pension plan, a special bonus to all workers, and the institution of a single restaurant for both executives and workers.

In the autumn of 1953 several foreigners joined us from overseas to help make the most of the increasing opportunities. Among them were Max Bladeck, who had been a militant Communist coal miner in the German Ruhr; Jens Wilhelmsen, a young Norwegian who had been a resistance fighter during the Nazi occupation of his country; and Frowin Junker, who had been a member of Hitler Youth.

The coming of Bladeck and his companions made possible further advances in replacing class-war thinking, not only in industry, but also in the political parties. There was a great interest among Japanese at that time in Germany, and Max and the others made the most of it. They paid visits to the executives of the National Railways Workers Union and the heads of other unions, including the Postal and Telecommunications Workers, and some of the top management and union executives of Toshiba, the Paper and Pulp Manufacturers' Association, the Heavy Electric Manufacturers' Association, and similar groups. They also addressed all forty-six prefectural governors for fifty minutes at the Governors' Conference. Twenty-four senior Diet Members from different parties met in one of the committee rooms to listen to them.

In December, the Shipbuilders' Association, the Metal Mining Association and the Steel Suppliers' Association all gave luncheons for the trio, followed by meetings at which they spoke. Next came a talk to 120 top officers of the National Rural Police. Perhaps the most significant event was a two-hour press conference with a

dozen editorial writers and city desk men from some of the big
dailies, many of whom had been influenced by Marxism. A digest
of the proceedings was sent to all newspapers in the country by
the hosts, the National Newspaper Association. The Japan Broadcasting Corporation also broadcast some of what Bladeck had to
say.

One of the men who was most gripped by Max Bladeck's story
of the change in his life and the impact of Moral Re-Armament on
the Communist Party in the Ruhr was Chief Justice Kotaro Tanaka.
He came to dinner and sat amazed as Max described the birth of
his Christian faith as he measured his life by absolute standards,
put right what he could and then saw with new eyes the inadequacy
of his Communist beliefs. Tanaka, the country's leading Catholic
layman, regarded Max thoughtfully when Max said, 'In Germany
it was the failure of Christians to live their convictions that enabled
us Communists to become the champions of the needed changes
in society.'

During that winter an opportunity arose in a different quarter
to replace Marxist philosophy with a more positive idea. After the
war the Occupation authorities had ordered school textbooks to
be rewritten in order to eliminate the nationalist teachings. Many
of the authors of the new books were Marxists and their thoughts
coloured the history and sociology texts. This autumn the Ministry
of Education decided to make some changes, including instructions
to all sociology teachers to inform their students about Moral Re-
Armament. Then they discovered that teachers had no adequate
material on MRA and asked us to prepare a 2,000-word article
for the Ministry's magazine, which went to all schools and colleges.
In line with this purpose we gave an interview to a professor who
was writing a book to be used by all sociology teachers. Later,
several textbooks were published for junior high school students,
introducing them to the concepts of MRA.

The New Year's vacation, during which all work stops in Japan,
enabled a hundred representatives of labour and management,
together with several Diet Members, to spend time together over
a long weekend at a hot springs in the Hakone Mountains. The
setting of a hot springs was ideal. After each session the men headed
for one communal bath and the women for another. Thick clouds
of steam partly shrouded a score of figures crouched in the very

hot water, only their heads visible, crowned with cold towels to dispel dizziness. Senators, company executives, labour leaders, all robbed of their trappings of rank, engaged in lively discussion of the topics raised at the meetings and expressed their most candid convictions. No one could emerge from that weekend without more real and open attitudes towards the others.

The presence of the wives of many of the Dietmen, business and labour leaders was a novel feature of the conference. It was most unusual for them to be included in any such gathering at that time. One industrialist who brought his wife said that in twenty-seven years, except to do the marketing and attend her father's funeral, she had not left the house. That had all changed since he went to Caux. It was heartening not only to have the women present, but to find them highly articulate.

A Toshiba delegation, headed by Tsunuke Takahashi, the Managing Director, spelled out their remarkable story of a new-found accord. Labour-management teams had come from other large electrical manufacturing companies. There was an atmosphere of miracles as many individuals spoke of their decisions involving alcohol, honesty with wives and new responsibilities as husbands and fathers. Mrs Togano, the Socialist Diet Member, summed up the feelings of many when she said, 'I did not really believe that what we experienced at Caux and Mackinac could happen in Japan. But it has.'

A visitor from California arrived early in the year and reinforced the campaign which Bladeck and his colleagues were waging. George Eastman was a prominent California businessman who had been President of the Los Angeles Chamber of Commerce. He came at a moment when the country was shaken by revelations of bribery involving some of the Cabinet and a number of Diet Members. It appeared that some of the large shipbuilding companies had been bribing politicians in order to obtain government contracts. As the investigation widened rumours flew and it seemed that the Yoshida government might be toppled. Other industries had been involved and there was considerable uneasiness in the business world, as well as in the Diet. In this situation George Eastman and Max Bladeck spoke forthrightly about honesty and the lack of it. From their backgrounds of capitalism and Communism they warned that democracy and freedom could not long survive if undermined by corruption. After Max and George had addressed the National Railways directors the Governor told our colleague Kataoka, who had been recently appointed Inspector General of the Railways, that they had better push ahead with Moral Re-Armament as their policy in preventing corruption and scandal in their organization.

Bladeck and Wilhelmsen were equally effective in addressing both the Right-wing and Left-wing Socialist Party conferences. They talked about the need for revolutionary change in human motives as the basis for a change in society. It was a breath of fresh air in a smoke-filled hall, and at both conferences they received more applause than any other speaker. Max also spoke to the executives of the Liberal Party – the power structure in the Government – and was well received by them, despite some very straight talking on his part. Bladeck, Wilhelmsen and Junker spent an evening with the top men of the Japan Broadcasting Corporation. Max was also asked to speak over short wave transmissions directed to the Soviet Union and Eastern Europe. He followed this with a nation-wide broadcast to the Japanese about the impact of MRA on the coal industry of Germany.

Max's last date before leaving Japan in mid-April was with Takano, Secretary General of the Trade Union Council, and the most powerful figure in Japanese labour. He had taken organized labour to the Left, and many believed he was a secret Communist. Max had more than an hour with him, telling him how he had been first a Socialist, then a Communist, and now had found a better ideology. Takano responded that he had a great respect for MRA because it created a moral discipline in men, and he understood it to be a progressive force.

While Eastman and Bladeck were speaking to these influential audiences, they were also taking part in a further series of industrial training meetings to enlarge the scope of the work begun at Toshiba. Among the companies which took part were Hitachi Shipbuilding, Ishikawajima Shipbuilding, Mitsubishi Electric, International Telephone and Telegraph and Mitsui Coal Mining – all giant enterprises.

Another significant development in the struggle to replace class war and labour-management confrontation was also taking place. Thanks to the spadework of Jens Wilhelmsen, Max and Katsuji Nakajima, firm friendships were built with a dynamic group of young Left-wing leaders. All were elected to the Upper House of the Diet after having become national chairmen of their powerful unions – the Coalminers, National Railwaymen, Telecommunications Workers, Postal Workers and Chemical Workers. Most of them were fiery, outspoken young men, strongly opposed to the conservative Government on most issues, and very suspicious of the United States. They were anti-Communist and each had fought the Communist Party's attempts to take control of their unions. But they were swayed at times by Communist propaganda in support of various causes.

Increasingly they came to MRA House, enjoying the comradeship with each other and with us, and the frank discussions over national and international issues. Among conservatives they were regarded as dangerous hot heads, but they were beginning to exert a positive influence among their Left-wing colleagues, holding a line against extremism and violence. The one whom I came to know the best was Tsuyoshi Suzuki, Chairman of the Telecommunications Workers. His life was typical of many during the turbulent post-war years.

Son of a small town postmaster, raised in a conservative Buddhist home, his life had been disrupted by the war. Drafted into the army, he had spent three unhappy years as part of the occupation force in Singapore. During that time his Tokyo home was destroyed by fire, his wife fled from the city to work on a farm, and his father died of malnutrition. When he returned to Tokyo he got a job as a Telecommunications worker, but his wife and children had to continue living in the countryside as there was no accommodation for them in Tokyo. Separated from his family, Suzuki went downhill and became a heavy drinker. He was deeply involved in work with the newly-formed union, which was being taken over by the Communists. Together with a colleague, Hitoshi Kubo, he ousted them from control, and from then on he was a prime target of Communist propaganda. His friend Kubo was elected to head the union and later Suzuki succeeded him.

Through Kubo he met Moral Re-Armament at the moment when they were deeply concerned about how to unite their divided union of some 200,000 members. Suzuki was impressed by the people he met in MRA and worked to raise finances to send Kubo to Mackinac. He and Kubo began to make progress in uniting the union by reconciling Right and Left-wing factions. A new discipline in Suzuki resulted in his wife and children coming to live with him in Tokyo. Since the beginning of the year he had been engaged in wage negotiations and had so convinced the Governor of Telecommunications of his integrity that the Governor supported the union's wage claims when he submitted them to the government for agreement.

To repay the hospitality the Eastmans had received Jean and I entertained a number of guests including Mr and Mrs Ishizaka over dinner. Ishizaka responded warmly to the news of all that George Eastman and Max had done and afterwards proposed to Ichimada that Ichimada call together a meeting of management men to consider the next steps to be taken in the country. Ichimada responded, and the occasion took place at the Bank of Japan guest house in May 1954. A dozen of the country's most powerful men, heads of banks and corporations, carried the ball. They evaluated what MRA was doing in Japan and urged practical support. Several of them talked about the new spirit of co-operation in their plants. Others spoke of the fight for honesty being waged to answer the spread of corruption in business and government. Among those who spoke were Ichimada, Ishizaka, Iwase, President of Mitsukoshi Department Store, Sodeyama, Chairman of Toyo Rayon, Hayakawa of Nippon Express, and Hori, head of the Fuji Spinning Company.

At the close of the year there was a significant meeting of five senior labour leaders – Yamahana, Chairman of the Chemical Workers; Suzuki, Chairman of the Telecommunications Workers; Yamamura, Chairman of the Heavy Electric Workers; Yokokawa, Chairman of the Postal Workers; and Yanagisawa. They came for lunch to plan for a two-day MRA labour conference to be held in early January at Atami Hot Springs. The conference was Yamahana's idea and the other men pitched in with him to make it the responsibility of all of them. More important than working out the details of the conference was the hammering out of their own convictions. All had been advocates of Marxism. Most of the afternoon was spent in our living room talking frankly about the giant task in which they were involved – to turn the philosophy of Sohyo, the voice of organized labour, from division to national unity, while still being faithful to the just claims of the union members for better conditions and wages.

The conference in Atami followed the pattern of the New Year gathering of the previous year, but was the product of the team-work of these men. Among those present were six Socialist Diet Members, the national chairmen of five unions and officials of fifteen other large unions whose members numbered more than one million. They explored the thought, 'As I am, so is my nation,' relating change at home and at work to new moral standards in the country. One of them, Aoki, Chairman of the Seamen's Union, summed it up when he said, 'We have got to deal with a spirit of bitterness in the labour movement. We are learning how to show humanity towards management as well as towards our workers.' On management's side, Nakahata, a senior negotiator for the National Railways, said, 'I was up against tougher railroad prob-lems than I could handle. Through Kozo Kimura I realized I was a very proud man and had the reputation of being too blunt in my dealings with the union, but I'm finding out in Hiroshima, where we have had the bitterest relations with the union, how to work with them to answer problems without conflicts.'

10

ENTERING THE NATIONAL ARENA

For Japan the summer of 1954 was a long hot one. The first of what became an annual wage offensive of the unions was bitter and lengthy and involved many areas of industry. Even more serious for the country was a political confrontation which paralyzed the Diet. Yoshida's government was determined to revive the national police system, scrapped by MacArthur. They felt that the division of the police into rural and metropolitan forces had made them ineffective in controlling crime and providing security against civil disorder. They wanted a centralized organization with greater powers, similar to Britain's Scotland Yard or America's FBI. The Left-wing and most intellectuals were bitterly opposed to what they felt was the beginning of a return to the repressive police state of the pre-war years.

The Liberal Party tried to push a Bill through the Diet before the session expired on May 22. Then the session was extended to early June and on the eve of voting on the Bill the Socialist Members resorted to staging a riot in the Lower House. Unable to prevent the measure from coming to a vote, they walked out in protest. The conservative coalition passed the Bill, while the Socialists claimed it had been illegally rammed through. The whole country was stirred up on the issue.

Another issue came to a boil during the spring and further divided Right and Left that summer. Yoshida succeeded in concluding a Mutual Defence Assistance Agreement with the United States after a full year of behind-the-scenes negotiations. In addition to the promise of mutual aid in maintaining the security and interests of the two countries, the pact contained several elements: the organization of modern Japanese armed forces on a small scale and strictly for purposes of national defence; the creation of a Defence Agency to control these forces; the centralization of the police system; and a Defence Secrets Protection Law to authorize security regulations. The Communists, Socialists and many others were alarmed by this international accord, some on pacifist grounds, fearing the rebirth of militarism, others resenting the mutual ties with the United States, which they felt violated Japan's strict neutrality. The Government argued that in the absence of adequate military defences against Russia and Communist China it was essential to maintain American protection.

Prime Minister Yoshida's championing of these changes in Occupation reforms was only part of his troubles. He alienated powerful elements opposed to his policies, but he also increasingly irritated many of his followers and supporters by his autocratic style and high-handed treatment of those who did not agree with him. He was breaking one of Japan's most treasured traditions, the behind-the-scenes consultations and compromises which led to consensus in political affairs as well as in every sphere. There was increasing talk among businessmen of seeking another premier. But many of the most responsible leaders of both Right and Left with whom we were in close touch proved to be a moderating influence in these divisions. While they often disagreed among themselves, they sought to resolve the disputes peacefully, successfully resisting the demands of the extremists.

However, the Government was plunged into further trouble in the autumn. Bribery scandals surfaced, involving Eisaku Sato, Secretary-General of the Liberal Party and others. Hatoyama was again bidding to unseat Yoshida. He had strengthened the Democratic Party, renaming it Progressive, and the coalition between them and the Liberals which Yoshida needed for a majority in the Diet was becoming shaky. Another leading contender for the premiership was Deputy Prime Minister Taketora Ogata, who had his own group of supporters and was finding it increasingly difficult to work with Yoshida. Yet another political boss, Tanzan Ishibashi, was also manoeuvring for power.

Now the Zaibatsu – the Mitsui, Sumitomo, Mitsubishi and other giant conglomerates – who had some influence in the selection of a premier, were again becoming restless about Yoshida and started to put pressure on him to resign. Yoshida, however, refused to budge. The Socialists saw this confusion as a great opportunity to gain power and push their demands to halt the American-Japanese alliance, strengthening of police and anti-labour laws. They also were vocal for the restoration of full diplomatic ties with the USSR and recognition of Communist China. The hand of the Left-wing was strengthened by a recession, as the rapid growth of basic industries had faltered.

From early November onwards, men who were at the heart of the political conflict talked with us about their concerns and we encouraged them to act together to resolve differences and restore public confidence in government. Ichimada was a close colleague of Yoshida; Hoshijima was prominent in the group who supported Hatoyama; Kozo Kimura was the intelligence adviser to Ogata and in personal touch with him each week. Ishizaka, Shibusawa, Tashiro, Moroi and others were in the front rank of the captains of industry who were active in political circles. And the Katos, Toganos, Yamahana and Kubo were at the heart of both Socialist Parties.

Ichimada came to dinner and we introduced him to Renzo Yanagisawa, the union head of Ishikawajima Shipyards. Renzo had been at Caux and Mackinac and impressed Ichimada with his stories of union leaders he had met who were working to make labour a positive force in other countries. He told him of his commitment to do the same in Japan and of the response he was having from both management and union at the shipyard. Kanju Kato came for lunch and talked about his priorities: first, in the political field, the uniting of the two Socialist Parties. There had been a growing conviction in both parties for such a move in order to oppose the government successfully. But, Kanju said, 'That is not an adequate motive for a merger. Unity must be based on moral principles, with constructive goals ahead of us.' Secondly, he was concerned about a major dispute then in progress between government and public employees unions – the postal workers, telephone and telegraph workers, National Railways workers, and others. 'That conflict must be solved on the basis of what is right,' he said. And he was co-operating with MRA friends who were heading these unions to try to do that. He went further: 'Industrial peace is essential for the Japanese economy, especially at this time of depression. And I am committed to fight for it at every opportunity I have.'

When we entertained Mr and Mrs Ishizaka at dinner the conversation ranged over the political and economic scenes and especially the part which senior management should play. We told him about the courageous efforts which Yanagisawa, Suzuki and others in the unions were making, and of Kanju and his friends in the Right-wing Socialist Party and men like Yamahana and Kubo in the Left-wing Party to improve the conditions of the workers without playing into the hands of the extreme Left. Yamahana had told us, 'Unemployment has now reached 800,000. If it gets to a million we will have a revolutionary situation on our hands, because the Communists are well prepared to exploit the hardship.'

Ishizaka said he and his friends were much concerned at the lack of leadership in the government and were putting pressure on the political chiefs to settle their differences. I had the impression that he would be glad to have Yoshida resign, but felt that Hatoyama was too liberal in his foreign policies, favouring recognition of Red China and closer ties with the Soviet. No manoeuvring for position was adequate to restore confidence, he said; government leaders must display some fresh and unselfish motives and better relation-ships between them. We encouraged him to work with Ichimada, Hoshijima and others who were committed to that fight.

A few days later, we were led closer to the heart of the govern-ment's problems. Kozo Kimura was in touch with us almost daily about his responsibilities. His boss, Deputy Premier Taketora Ogata, was virtually running the government, while Yoshida had gone into seclusion while making up his mind whether or not to resign. Then Yoshida asked Ogata to prepare a report on public opinion about the political crisis, an analysis of the over-all national situation and recommendations on how to proceed. Ogata told Kimura to draft the paper. He came to us to get any ideas we had. Four of us sat down to lunch – Kozo, Kataoka, Director of the National Railways, Toyo Sohma and I. Kimura was frank about the bitter rivalry between Yoshida and Hatoyama, and the ambitions of Ogata and Ishibashi to succeed to the premiership. He had evidence of the public's loss of confidence in the conservative leaders and of the growing threat of class war. He talked, too, of the lure of Peking to the intelligentsia and some labour leaders in the face of government disunity and the inability of industry to raise the wages of workers or increase employment.

Out of our discussion several points emerged: the need for

conservative leaders to settle their animosities; the priority of finding positive policies on which political and business leaders could unite to improve the economy; and the initiation of open-hearted diplomacy towards Japan's former enemies, especially the Philippines and Korea, in order to reopen the closed door of these countries. We urged Kozo to deal boldly with his boss in helping him to set the pace in creating unity with his colleagues and rivals.

Kimura submitted his report to Ogata and asked for the opportunity to talk further about some of his recommendations. Ogata invited him to lunch, at which Kozo told his boss about major changes in his life, especially his commitment to serve others, rather than put his own career first. This led to his telling about Moral Re-Armament and its outreach in the world. Ogata said he would like to meet people at MRA House. We invited him to dinner and he sent word he could come four days later. On that day, late in November, the political crisis had deepened and the newspapers were full of rumours about the departure of Yoshida and speculation on who his successor to the premiership would be. It looked like a close race between the three men – Hatoyama, Ogata and Ishibashi.

Punctually at 6.30, Ogata's big black limousine swept through the gates of MRA House, tailed by several press cars. The reporters had been following the Deputy Prime Minister wherever he went, trying to question him on the latest political developments. Ogata stepped quickly into the house and the front doors closed, leaving the pressmen standing around to ponder the significance of Ogata's visit to MRA. He was a genial man with an appearance of quiet confidence. He proved a good listener that evening and weighed his words carefully. Jean and I had included at dinner Kimura, Katsuji Nakajima, Toyo and Tokiko Sohma, and a few other colleagues. We stayed away from any talk about the political crisis and concentrated on inspiring our guest with answers to problems in Japan and other parts of the world. Katsuji told Ogata of his liberation from his hatred of America and finding a better way than Marxism; we spoke of the new-found understanding between Ichimada and Yanagisawa, of Schuman and Adenauer and other examples of teamwork displacing division. Ogata seemed most responsive. During the next months we were in touch with him directly, as well as through Kimura. Behind the scenes he made genuine efforts to resolve the personal rivalries among his colleagues.

Shortly after this dinner I was confronted with the opportunity to meet Hatoyama. Hearing about Ogata's visit, Hoshijima said he wanted me to meet Hatoyama. He felt I could give him some valuable ideas and that Hatoyama was open to receiving them. I hesitated before accepting, because Hatoyama was the most controversial figure in the country and his every move was watched. However, I appreciated the chance to meet this man. Hatoyama had suffered the indignity of being purged during the Occupation. He had had a major stroke, walked with a cane and used a wheelchair. He tired quickly, was far from robust and some questioned whether he could shoulder the burdens of the premiership. Although his speech was slow, his mind was quick and he had the reputation of being a formidable adversary. He was bitter toward Yoshida because he felt the latter had cheated him out of the highest post some years earlier. Now he seemed determined at all costs to secure what he felt was his rightful place.

Hoshijima arranged the meeting on the morning of December 7 in the house where Hatoyama received many callers. Hoshijima, Yukika and Toyo accompanied me. Hatoyama welcomed us politely and sat looking at me intently as Hoshijima introduced us. He had searching eyes behind large glasses, a round face, large ears, a sloping forehead and thinning hair. After Hoshijima had spoken briefly about our work, Hatoyama turned to me. I said I appreciated his taking time to see us at such a busy time. I had been praying for him amidst the pressures of the decisions he had to make. (He was a Christian.) As a foreigner, I had no part in Japanese politics, but I had been led into the lives and concerns of some who bore heavy responsibilities and so understood a little of the great issues at stake.

Then I spoke about America, of how our failure to live our Christian faith led to materialism and division from which other countries as well as ourselves had suffered. I had recognized that I was part of the problem and had decided to change and try to live by God's will. I had found it to be true that honest apology was the key to honest peace. Schuman of France and Adenauer of Germany had proved that unity could spring from trust, even in humanly impossible situations. Some of Hatoyama's fellow Diet

106

Members had opened the hearts of Congressmen and Americans from coast to coast by their sincere apologies. On the other hand, disunity between leaders of the free world had opened the doors to Communism. I quoted Ulbricht, head of Communist East Germany, who had recently boasted that democracy would not survive in Japan and its people would soon turn to Marxism. Hatoyama thanked me courteously for coming and we left. I was uncertain whether I had been too brash in my remarks, but when I next saw him he was very cordial.

Thanks in part to our senior friends, the political scene soon began to clear. Business leaders prevailed on Yoshida to resign and go into retirement. Ogata surprised his countrymen by withdrawing from contention for the premiership. Hatoyama emerged as the winner over Ishibashi and was chosen by his party as the new Prime Minister. The conservative parties – Liberal and Progressive – entered the campaign for the February elections somewhat less divided than they had been and scored a fairly easy victory over the two Socialist parties. After the elections there was a growing pressure on both conservatives and socialists to unite their parties and in October the two Socialist Parties did merge. Our colleagues had a hand in the development, as Shidzue and Kanju described it to us privately.

When Kanju had first returned from Mackinac, a changed man, he had apologized to the Left-wing leaders for his ambitious rivalry. But despite his efforts in 1952, the Right- and Left-wings had drawn further apart. Kanju would normally have gone with the Left-wing, but its leaders' quarrels were too much for him and he threw in his influence with the Right-wing. His first step was to go with Shidzue to talk with the Right-wing leader, Kawakami, who had been so discouraged by the disunity among the Socialists that he had resigned. The Katos talked with the Kawakamis in their home and ended by being quiet and seeking God's direction about their responsibilities. Kawakami reluctantly agreed to accept the chairmanship of the Right-wing again. Then, at the recent conference of the two parties to talk about their unity, Kawakami declined to run for any position in a united party and his unselfish leadership was a major factor in bringing the two parties together.

The merging of the two conservative parties, with their several rival cliques, was no easy task, but in November, one month after

107

the Socialists united, the Liberal Democratic Party was born. It was an event of some significance, since the party became for more than a quarter century the relatively stable foundation for government. Here, too, Hoshijima, Ichimada and other friends were effective reconcilers of the intra-party ambitions and factions.

It was becoming clear that MRA was as effective a catalyst in politics as in industry. Those who applied its principles were liable to find themselves in centres of conflicts, but often able to create trust and co-operation among opponents. So, during this time some of them who were the most responsible in national affairs began to meet every couple of weeks in a 'cabinet' session. They were, perhaps, a counterpart of the 'clubs' which wielded power in the political parties and business circles, except that this group was composed of widely differing interests, rather than representing any clique.

At these meetings, held in MRA House, they talked over the issues which were most on their minds. At the first session, for example, among the topics discussed were: the role of the National Railways in uniting the country (Kataoka); how to get government officials and public service employees who were in MRA to fight for a changed attitude in the National Trade Union Council towards industrial relations (Yanagisawa); with Communist China stepping up its 'peace offensive,' it was urgent to bring unity to Japan's political leaders (Kimura); and how to reach the intellectuals who wrote for the influential magazines (Yamahana).

A little later, Diet Members took a similar step. During sessions of the Diet they found it difficult to make time in their offices to talk with each other or with those of us with whom they wanted to confer. So they arranged to have a breakfast every Tuesday morning at MRA House at which they could talk over their mutual concerns and seek guidance together on matters both personal and public. It was the one place, they said, where conservatives and Socialists could talk candidly with each other and seek a common mind. It became a significant arena for battling out positive inter-party strategies.

These opportunities for forming common policies were timely. We had embarked on an ambitious project late in the autumn of 1954 which took us publicly into the main stream of political and business affairs. While the Japanese delegation to Caux were visiting London that summer they saw a performance of an MRA play, *The Boss*, and felt it would have a powerful message for Japan. Its theme was that democracy needed a moral backbone in homes and factories in order to stand against the lure of militant Marxism. A businessman's home and plant were the scene of action and although the setting was Western, the Japanese felt the play spoke loud and clear to their countrymen.

On their return, it was decided to mount the play if an adequate cast could be put together. Yukika Sohma and Sen Nishiyama set about translating the script. We held a number of readings to try out candidates to play the eight characters in the cast, and spent time together discussing what the play was all about. It came as a shock to our friends that they might appear on stage. Most of them were at first stilted and artificial when they tried out for the parts. Gradually, as they lived into the characters they began to come to life. Then we had a lucky break. Tone Kimura's uncle, Takashi Sugawara, who had recently been honoured by *Mainichi* as the dramatic director of the year, was invited by Tone to read *The Boss* and come to a rehearsal. He was interested in the play and over dinner became fascinated when we outlined for him the purpose we had in mind for its use. We told him we believed that a fundamental issue in Japan in the 1950's was the struggle for a free democracy. *The Boss* could strengthen the resolve of businessmen, union officials, politicians and others to make democracy work. We envisaged a series of performances for such audiences.

Sugawara said this was just the kind of role the theatre should play in society, and offered to help with its direction. From December onwards he went to work with skill and patience. Because our aim was ideological we tried to select individuals whose jobs would make their acting especially significant. The role of the industrialist was played by Kataoka, now one of the top officials in the National Railways. The union leader was played by Yanagisawa, head of the Ishikawajima Shipyard Workers Union. Both took considerable persuading, because they felt inept on stage and both were extremely busy men. But what they lacked in acting skills they made up in understanding of the characters they played. The part of an undercover Communist union official went to Takagi, a young staff worker on a Socialist periodical, with a Marxist background, now committed to MRA.

During January and February, 1955, we visited most of our friends in the top rank of management – Ishizaka, who had just been named Chairman of a newly-created National Productivity Council; Takeshi Kajii, Governor of the Telecommunications Corporation; Yamagiwa, new Governor of the Import-Export Bank; Eikichi Araki, who had been Ambassador to Washington and was now Governor of the Bank of Japan in place of Ichimada; Tashiro, the most prominent man in textiles; Yanagita, President of Japan Air Lines; Sato, President of the Mitsui Bank; Asahara, President of Nissan Motors; Ishikawa, President of the Federation of Economic Organizations. These were key figures in the drive to reinvigorate the economy. They grappled with wider issues than those involved in managing their own giant organizations – who were the men they should support for top positions in the government? Had the time come to push for trade with the Soviet and Communist China? Which industries should be given preference in the allotment of scarce capital? What should be the strategy of the large companies in confronting Sohyo's spring wage offensive?

As we met with these men we told them about the play *The Boss*, and offered to arrange a preview for a select group in order to give them a chance to evaluate it and, hopefully, to make use of it in their industries and the country at large. After checking with a dozen of them, we decided on February 16 and 18 for 'sneak previews'. As there would only be about a dozen people at each occasion we staged the performance very informally in our living room at MRA House. The men came for an early dinner, immediately followed by the show. Between the dining room and the living room was a wide arch across which a curtain was drawn. The cast came quietly into the living room, with its furniture rearranged to form the set, which was the living room in the Boss's house. The curtain was pulled open and an enterprise was launched which was to make its impact not only on business executives, but on the Cabinet, as well as thousands of workers' homes.

The two dozen men who were at these previews were the most powerful in banking and industry. Among them were the chairmen of the two largest national employers' associations, the presidents of the Mitsui Bank, the largest insurance company, Japan Air Lines, coal mining, metal mining, shipbuilding and heavy electrical manufacturing companies, the president of the Japan-American

Society, managing director of the largest motion picture company and, for good measure, the Chief of Staff of the Defence Forces and the Commanding General of the Ground Forces.

The audience was bowled over by the play. They had probably been expecting a competent amateur production. They were hit by a powerful ideological weapon which was also a gripping human tale. Several of them had tears on their faces, moved by the drama of a husband and wife, father and son, boss and union head. At the end of the performance for the first audience, Ishizaka, their acknowledged leader, rose to his feet: 'When we in our company helped our people in management and the union to travel to Caux we made a great investment. At Toshiba, for example, one of our gatekeepers, Yamamura, went as a chairman of the union. That man has been transformed. He has now risen to become chairman of the national union.

'I want to congratulate Mr Yanagisawa, whom you saw act so well on stage, and Mr Doko (Yanagisawa's boss at Ishikawajima Shipyards, who was in the audience) for the outstanding way they have solved their management-labour conflicts and produced an example of co-operation for our industries. This play is the result of Peter Howard's inspiration and, behind him, of the world figure of Frank Buchman, whom I met at Caux and whose genius has produced Moral Re-Armament.

'As you know, I recently accepted the position of Chairman of the National Productivity Centre because I wanted to work, not just to rationalize our industries, but to create national teamwork. I have talked about this with the Minister of Labour and like me, he has great expectations of MRA. I am sure, after this evening, you are thinking that *The Boss* is good for your industry. But please realize too that it is good for the whole nation.'

Ishizaka could not have sounded a clearer note. Now we had to get behind him and his colleagues and help them put the play to best possible use. Four days later, we had a third preview, mainly for leaders in the textile industry. We immediately followed up these previews by visits with Ishizaka and the rest to encourage their initiative. They decided that *Keidanren*, the Federation of Economic Organizations, as the top business institution, should officially sponsor seven performances of *The Boss*, four of them in the theatre on the top floor of the Daiichi Building, which had been MacArthur's headquarters, in the heart of the financial district. They were set for late March and April. On each evening a different senior businessman would introduce the play: Ishizaka, Ishikawa, Yanagita (President of Japan Air Lines), and so on. Yamagiwa, Governor of the Import-Export Bank, accepted the responsibility for raising the funds needed for building the set, renting the theatres, printing invitations and tickets, and the like. Officials at *Keidanren* would work with us in allocating tickets to representatives of business and to key individuals in all walks of life.

We gave similar previews of the play for Socialists and labour men on Sunday at the House. They arrived at 1.30 for an all-afternoon meeting, had dinner and saw the show. Among them were five Left-wing Senators, the national chairmen of five large unions. At the meeting we talked frankly about the personal commitment, discipline and courage required to create teamwork and unity. Katsuji, Yanagisawa and Yamamura fought straight on the point that neither Capitalism nor Marxism had cured the ambition, jealousy and materialism in human nature, and that a more fundamental moral revolution was necessary if society was to be transformed. *The Boss* seemed to draw as great a response from these men as it had from the businessmen. They, too, were eager for the play to be used among the members of their party and unions.

The showings of *The Boss* proved an effective stroke. The audiences were made up of key personnel from many large business firms, both management and labour, as well as Diet Members, several of the Imperial Family, and representatives of the news media and education. A number of those who saw the play wanted to arrange performances for their own organizations. Our concern was to concentrate on the most significant opportunities. Kozo Kimura was convinced that the Prime Minister should have the chance to see the play, and talked with us, along with Hoshijima, about how to arrange a performance for the Cabinet. Then they quietly went to work.

We had got to know Hatoyama's daughter and son-in-law, the Furusawas. He was a director of the Bank of Japan. His wife, a charming lady, responded enthusiastically to *The Boss*. She and her mother had a key part in clinching the event. I had seen

Atami, January 1955. A lively conversation takes place in the hot spring between three presidents of national unions: Nishimaki (Seamen), Nagaoka (National Railway Workers) and Diet Member Yamahana (Chemical Workers).

Socialist Diet Members Kanju Kato (R) and Hideo Yamahana (L) talk over a *hibachi* at the Atami MRA Conference, 1955.

Governor Shinji Sogo, of the Japan National Railways, who pioneered the fastest train in the world, The Dream Express, capable of 250km/hour, takes his leave at the MRA Assembly, Caux.

An early version of the high speed trains

In the Japanese Diet Building Yahachi Kawai, Speaker of the Upper House, addresses members of the MRA World Mission prior to their welcome on the floor of the Senate, June 1955. To his right is Ole Bjorn Kraft, former Foreign Minister of Denmark; to his left is Dr Oscar Leimgruber, Chancellor of Switzerland 1943-51.

Prime Minister Hatoyama's official residence, with the Diet Building in the background, where the production of "The Boss" was staged

A scene from "The Boss". In the role of the union leader (left) Yanagisawa, head of the Ishikawajima Shipyards Union; in the role of the manager (right) Kataoka, senior official in the National Railways

Hatoyama when Jean and I were invited to the Prime Minister's annual cherry blossom viewing in Shinjuku Gardens and had the opportunity to say a few words about *The Boss* and hoped that he and his colleagues could see it. He said he had heard a lot about the play and would like to.

A week later, the Furusawas came for dinner and told us her father had just told them that he and his Cabinet and a few top party officials were ready to see the play next day in his official residence. He would end the Cabinet meeting early, around noon, and invite his ministers to adjourn to a large room in the building to see *The Boss*. We had been alerted for this development and had adapted the set for a small stage and had a curtain ready. All of our cast managed to get leave from their work. Despite some grumbling among some of the Cabinet, they trooped in. Foreign Minister Mamoru Shigemitsu was one who had seen the play and he had added his word that it was a significant play and one which men in public life should experience.

A crowd of reporters and the camera crews of the three national TV networks were in the hall, when Hatoyama entered in his wheel chair with his colleagues. As soon as they were settled, our international chorus stepped in front of the curtain and sang three songs in Japanese. Sumi Mitsui gave a brief introduction to the play, stressing that it had had an impact on the lives and thinking of many people in Europe and America. After the final curtain Kataoka and Yanagisawa spoke briefly, relating the theme of the play to their own lives and work. Then they introduced the cast to the Prime Minister.

Although this audience of seasoned politicians was the most sophisticated one to have seen *The Boss*, the reaction seemed genuinely enthusiastic. Shigemitsu and Ichimada, now Finance Minister, were among those who responded to the suggestion that a performance should be arranged for a larger number of Diet Members. Sugawara, who had done so much through his direction to perfect the production, had sat quietly watching the faces in the audience and listening to the comments afterwards. He came to me and said, 'This showing is truly an event of historic importance in Japanese theatre. It fulfils the purest purpose of the stage – to mirror for men life at its best, so that they can apply the truths it communi-

113

cates. And today those who saw it can carry its message into the heart of the nation's life.'

The newspaper and TV reported the occasion prominently. One network commentator remarked, 'The story of *The Boss* is that a spiritual revolution is the answer to a materialist revolution. No wonder the Prime Minister listened so intently, since the theme is so relevant to Japan.'

INTERLUDE:

GENERALS, TYCOONS AND OTHERS

During our first three years in Tokyo the American military presence was almost as pervasive as it had been during the Occupation. The fighting in Korea, followed by military deadlock, made the naval and air bases in Japan of the greatest importance, and even after the Korean threat diminished, confrontation with Soviet Russia and Communist China ensured that the United States maintained its strength in Japan and Okinawa. The attitude towards the American military had changed since the Occupation ended and its presence had become a divisive factor in the country. The Yoshida Government held firmly to the terms of the Security Treaty, recognizing that the United States lifted most of the burden of national defence from its shoulders. Most of the business and financial community also appreciated the large volume of trade developed by the procurement programme of goods and services required by the armed forces. In hindsight, this economic boom was a crucial prelude to Japan's economic recovery and expansion, since it provided both a market for basic industries and a fund of dollars with which to purchase essential imports.

On the other hand, large segments of the population were increasingly opposed to the military. Left-wing extremists were passionately determined to break the ties with America so that Japan might follow a neutralist or pro-Communist foreign policy. Farmers were resentful of the building of large military air bases which deprived them of good agricultural land. Many were fearful of their country's involvement in a nuclear war. Yet others, with no political concerns, were becoming irritated by the criminal conduct of some servicemen.

Our contact with the American military ranged from entertaining GIs on furlough from Korea at MRA House to visits with senior generals. During the Occupation our concern was that the military understand our programme and allow us full freedom to operate. Later, we tried to help them improve their relations with the Japanese. When our family arrived in Japan, General MacArthur's place as Supreme Commander had been taken by General Matthew Ridgway, a very different personality with a reputation as a hard-working, punctilious, shrewd man, with little of MacArthur's flamboyance. Senator Alexander Smith had given Jean and me a letter of introduction to him. He received us in his office and asked what he could do for us.

I told him about the dinner we had had with Senators Smith and Sparkman and the Japanese. Ridgway asked how we had been able to get that influential group together and I told him of the first large delegation to Caux and the others which followed. He was especially interested in the change in Kanju and Shidzue Kato and other Socialists, whose anti-American attitudes concerned him. He asked about our aims in the country, and when we said that our Japanese friends were convinced that Japan must have a moral and spiritual basis on which the democratic constitution could be secure and flourish, he heartily agreed.

Ridgway wanted to know who was active in MRA and how we were doing with the negative intellectuals. Then he said that while his understanding of MRA was amorphous, it seemed an essential approach to the world's problems. Wars, he said, settle nothing, though they had to be fought when savages threatened civilization. Without a foundation of faith and moral and spiritual force there would be an endless repetition of violence. He asked if we would return for a longer briefing at which he would include members of his staff.

At this second briefing the General asked Jean and me shrewd questions designed to draw us out to educate his staff officers. He first asked me to summarize Moral Re-Armament's work in Japan and in the world. I hit some of the highlights, including Yoshida's backing of the first delegation to Caux; the response to them from Adenauer and the US Congress; and the successive attempts of Japanese travelling abroad to regain the trust of former enemies.

'If I were put on the stand to give my impression of what you have told me,' Ridgway responded, 'would I be right in saying Moral Re-Armament's aim is to create integrity in personal and private life through basic Christian principles?'

We told him he was right, but that a distinctive characteristic of Buchman's work was to put Christianity in simple language everybody could understand – essential in a non-Christian country like Japan. Strict Presbyterianism, for example, was not the most suitable medium for mediating great truths to Japanese Marxists.

'But if you don't use Christian terms, what do you use?' We spoke about moral absolute standards, being quiet and listening to your inner voice, and the changes in character that may result.

'Then, don't people interpret the standards according to their own ideas, unless you speak to them of the character of Jesus Christ?' We talked more about absolute standards and how in fact they embody the Sermon on the Mount and serve as an introduction to the personality of Christ.

The General wanted to know, 'Where do you actually begin with the Japanese?' So we went into the heart of the philosophy of change – Be quiet and see what in your life is not absolute; give as much of your life as you know to as much of God as you understand; put right what you can and watch what revolutionary results begin to happen around you through the working of God's spirit.

'What do you say to Communists, who have no use for God?' We said, we tell them they are not revolutionary enough, and described how German Communist coal miners responded to the thought of a missing factor in Marxism – a revolutionary change in the human heart and will, the only satisfactory basis for world change.

Ridgway had one more question: 'How can we come over here and try to help the Japanese clean house, while in Washington our own house is in unsavoury disorder?' 'That's a very good question,' we said. MRA is concerned with the whole world, and while a few of us were here in Japan many more were fighting the battle on the home front in the United States. As we left, he thanked us warmly, said he had no reservations about what we were doing and would follow our programme with the greatest interest.

We maintained our friendship with senior American officers as best we could, as well as getting to know a number of GIs. In 1954, with public feeling mounting against American troops, a couple with whom we had made friends during a time of unhappiness in their marriage led us again into the heart of the military.

They introduced Jean and me to their friends, Colonel and Mrs Stephan. He was in charge of Information-Education for the troops stationed in the Tokyo area. As a former I and E officer, I understood some of his problems. Belatedly, the Pentagon and top brass in Tokyo were focussing on the conduct and character of the military personnel stationed overseas. They realized how important it was to avoid ugly incidents which would be used by anti-American elements, and also to help the GI to appreciate the citizens and way of life of the country in which he found himself. But how to do it? The training programmes were unimaginative and often not put into effect by the commanders of units who felt there were more urgent priorities.

Colonel Stephan became interested in what I told him about my work in Europe during World War II and asked for ideas for his programme. One evening at the House I introduced him to Katsuji Nakajima, who told him about his hatred of Americans after his Hiroshima bomb experience and his changed feelings about the United States. Stephan was impressed and asked Nakajima and me to brief the men who were responsible for leading orientation discussions among the troops. So Katsuji and I met with these men, told them our story and gave them ideas and material for their training programme, which that month centred around how to live effectively as representatives of America in Japan.

Stephan carried the project a step further. He invited me to lunch at the officers' mess at Pershing Heights, the GHQ of US Forces in the Far East. We met a number of his fellow officers, including the Chief of Staff, General Christenberry. He and his deputy, General Stuart, came to dinner at MRA House. At the meal also were George Eastman and Max Bladeck. The generals asked if we could be prepared to lead the regular Information-Education meeting next month for the two thousand officers stationed in the Tokyo area and at GHQ. The subject designated for the month was the 'character and conduct' of the military. We happily accepted and proposed that George, Max, Jens Wilhelmsen and I should speak together and emphasize 'character and conduct in an ideological age'.

There were six compulsory one-hour meetings held to cover the whole group. The first session took place at nine o'clock in the morning in the Ernie Pyle Theatre in downtown Tokyo. As we sat on the high stage, looking down on the rows of officers waiting in gloomy silence, I wondered if we had bitten off more than we could chew. The officers, we had been told, disliked being summoned from their busy routine to a lecture which some of them regarded as a waste of time. General Christenberry had announced that he would chair the meeting, so the officers had come in larger numbers than usual. The General introduced us and called on me to run the meeting. The sleepy and bored faces came to life when I sketched Max's Communist background and Max, interpreted by Jens, described how Jens, as a youth staying in his home, won him over to a superior ideology.

The audience remained gripped during the hour-long presentation and the same thing happened at the next five sessions. Afterwards, the generals and colonels who had introduced us said these were not only the largest, but also the most responsive audiences in the entire programme. The commanding general wrote me a letter of citation, expressing the thanks of his command for 'the very valuable service rendered in providing essential training'.

A very different American encounter was with John D. Rockefeller III and his wife. Rockefeller had a great personal interest in Japan, had financial interests in the country and had made a number of visits, including official governmental missions. He was concerned with Japan's economic recovery, but also with her cultural and educational development. His contacts had been almost entirely with business and cultural leaders and conservative politicians. He had had little opportunity to meet Socialists or labour leaders or to have direct touch with those who were criticial of America. The previous year I had met his lawyer, Don McLean, who travelled with him to Japan and helped arrange his appointments. I had given McLean a picture of our work with the Left-wing and he had said he wished Rockefeller could meet some of them privately, when the Rockefellers were next in Tokyo. I met them through McLean in the lobby of the Imperial Hotel. We talked briefly and I invited them to dinner at the House to meet a few of our Socialist friends. They accepted.

A dozen of us sat down to dinner that Sunday evening. Jean and I had included Diet Member Yamahana, who was also Chairman of the Chemical Workers; Kanju Kato; Yamamura, head of the Toshiba union; and Senator Kubo, Chairman of the Telecommunications Workers. Yukika Sohma provided simultaneous translation in both languages. John Rockefeller was a quiet, unassuming, shy man and listened more than he talked. During the evening the conversation ranged over the Japanese scene – political, economic and social – but also the international situation. The Socialists were polite, but very outspoken about their convictions. Rockefeller drew them out on why they feared or disliked American policy. Yamahana and Kubo both spoke appreciatively of what they had experienced through MRA, and Yamamura told about the revolution at Toshiba, which he said was making class war out of date.

Kanju Kato was the only one who was somewhat belligerent, saying it was difficult to trust America's motives for her military and economic ties with Japan. Max Bladeck joined in, maintaining that both countries, along with the whole democratic world, must turn to a moral ideology. Rockefeller asked many questions and seemed to take even the uncomfortable answers in his stride. Next day an enormous bouquet of flowers came from the couple, with a note saying how much they had enjoyed the evening. McLean told me later that they said it was the most interesting and instructive time they had spent in Japan.

We also had an encounter with a couple who had a similar standing to the Rockefellers in Japan. Rowland Harker and Don Libby, a young American who had joined our team in Tokyo, were spending a few days resting in the mountains. There they met a fellow hiker and Don introduced himself in his limited Japanese and the two started a halting conversation. A frail and slightly awkward figure, the middle-aged stranger seemed very shy, but Don did his best to draw him out.

'What is your name?' Don finally asked.

'Sumitomo.'

He invited them to his impressive home nearby and they learned that he was Kichizaemon Sumitomo, head of the family which had owned the great business and industrial empire. Rowland was well aware of the man's status, but Don continued asking him questions, much to Rowland's embarrassment.

'What is your work?' he wanted to know.

'Oh, I don't really have any work.'

'Are you retired?'

'Well, yes, perhaps.'

Back in Tokyo, when Don told us of the encounter, we encouraged him to get in touch with his friend, and Jean and I were invited, along with Yasu and Yukika, to visit him and his family one Sunday in their home on a hill near Kamakura. Kichizaemon and Haruko and their two young daughters were all very shy, but gradually thawed and began to ask questions about us and our work, and we were able to draw them out about themselves.

Until the Occupation authorities divested him of control of the companies and much of his property, Kichizaemon Sumitomo had lived like royalty. Much later, when I had got to know him well, we were talking about the price of an article and he said hesitantly, 'I don't really know much about what things cost. I never used money.' He went on to explain that if he visited a store and something took his fancy – a piece of jade or an automobile – he would tell an attendant he wanted it and walk away.

Although much of the Sumitomo fortune had been confiscated, a good deal remained. One time, after he had mentioned a home of his I had not heard of, I asked how many homes he had. Sumitomo looked confused and began counting and murmured, 'Seven – I think.' One of these homes, in Kyoto, was a small palace, a national museum which contained a fabulous collection of jade and other treasures.

When we began to assemble a Caux delegation, I asked Kichizaemon and Haruko if they would like to join it. After much hesitation, Kay (as he asked us to call him) timidly agreed. It was a big step for both of them, as they shrank from publicity and he, especially, even from close social contacts. Then he had to fight through a protective cordon of Sumitomo advisers and officials who were concerned lest he make some unfortunate public statement that might bring dishonour to the Sumitomo name. He took me to meet several of these men, some of them presidents of Sumitomo companies, others were elderly advisers. The latter were jealous of any intrusion on the influence they had exercised over Sumitomo ever since he was a boy, when his father had died. Despite his shy and faltering manner, Kay showed great pertinacity, and Haruko proved to have a will of iron once she had made up her mind about something.

They travelled with us, with their two daughters, to Caux and afterwards through the Ruhr, Paris and London and across the

States. The Sumitomo name was a door opener. Kay was giving much thought to the Sumitomo companies and what part they might play in the development of the country. It was a delicate matter, since officially he was now dissociated entirely from control or policy making. But he wanted the Sumitomo empire to become a pattern for other industries, in the integrity of their dealings, their relationship with labour and in concern for society.

On their return, Kay and Haruko went into action with the presidents of the companies. They gave a formal luncheon to which fourteen company heads came, together with senior advisers. Kay apologized for irresponsibility and apathy about the companies, as well as about the life of the nation. At Caux, he said, they had decided to live in a way that would help to answer class war. They had got to know and become friends with Socialists and labour leaders. They believed that the Sumitomo companies had a distinctive role in the country. This event led to a visit to Osaka and Kyoto a month later in which the Sumitomo men took responsibility for the main events – a dinner for a number of top Sumitomo executives, a meeting in the Osaka Club for senior businessmen and a similar meeting in Kyoto. It was the start of a significant entry into some of the most powerful industries in the country.

Accompanying the Sumitomos on the Caux delegation were two women whom we had recently met and who were also to lead us into a potent area of Japanese life. One day two elderly ladies paid a visit to MRA House, introduced by Hoshijima. Their looks were deceptive. They were short and chubby, grandmotherly types, whose mild appearance concealed a pair of fiery spirits. Mrs Hide Inouye, now in her early eighties, had been president of Japan Women's University, an institution among whose alumnae were the wives of many prominent men of affairs. Mrs Hiro Ohashi, in her seventies, was the present university president. They were nationally known for their pioneering in women's education, but more than that, they had become symbols to thousands of their former students of moral integrity and social justice.

The ladies asked if they might join the delegation to Caux and in due course set off in high spirits. They won the hearts of all they met. Frank Buchman called them his *kokeshi* dolls, an apt description of their round figures, bright eyes and cheerful disposition. Despite their age, they were always in the van of any enterprise – whether touring an assembly line, speaking at a meeting or calling on civic dignitaries.

On their return to Tokyo they opened many doors. They called on the Minister of Education, whom they knew well, to encourage him in a programme of citizenship training in schools. They supported the efforts of the Sumitomos to enlighten their company executives, since a number of the latter were married to their alumnae. On the occasion of the 50th anniversary of the founding of Japan Women's University they held a two-hour meeting for the graduates, gathering from around the country, at which Jean and I were the main speakers. A few days later, the two ladies brought a selected group of sixty-five alumnae to the House for training in 'How to change and inspire people.'

Not long afterwards we encountered another memorable character. Russia had begun slowly returning Japanese prisoners captured in Manchuria at the end of World War II. The first to arrive were those who had been successfully indoctrinated and were being sent back as agents or enthusiastic for the cause of Communism. They were followed by the majority, who were indifferent. Then came finally those who had been involved in military intelligence or who were labelled anti-Communists. In early February, 1957, Tokiko Sohma had word that her brother, Tatsuji Seki, was to be among the next group of returnees. When he was taken prisoner he was a member of an Army intelligence unit and so had been held for eleven years. During that time his wife and daughter had died, leaving a teenage son.

Soon after his return, Seki came to dinner with us. His gaunt figure, nervous speech and gestures revealed the strain, privations and dangers he had endured. He had a vivid story to tell. Like most of the hundreds of thousands of fellow prisoners, he had been taken to Siberia. Thousands had died amidst the cold and primitive living conditions. After a while he had been included in working parties on construction sites and had some enlightening insights into Russian life. He had been moved from one community to another and everywhere he had seen the countryside dotted with half-completed buildings. The local officials, he said, had received grants from Moscow for the construction of factories and offices, but because of incompetence or graft the funds had run out before the projects had been completed. Dishonesty was everywhere. The

123

Arnett Branch Library,
310 Arnett Blvd.
Rochester, N. Y. 14619

Japanese soon found they could not put down a hammer or shovel and turn their backs without it being stolen. The keys to the prison camp storehouses were always given to the prisoners, never to the Russian guards, otherwise food and tools soon disappeared.

Seki had read an article about Caux in a Russian newspaper. The story was negative, but it gave sufficient detail of an international force at work, dedicated to living by absolute moral standards and the remaking of society, so that he had decided that if released he would try to seek out Moral Re-Armament. To his astonishment and delight he found that his sister was giving her full time to the work and he said he wanted to have a part. With Seki was a companion, Tomiji Iseda, who had shared his tribulations and had returned with him. The two of them were to become effective fighters in the battles for a sound nation.

11

TWO FRIENDLY INVASIONS

After the series of opening performances of *The Boss*, the play was given for educators, the National Railways and for Diet Members. Then performances were halted in order to prepare for a new development. Ole Björn Kraft, former Foreign Minister of Denmark, proposed to Frank Buchman that he, Kraft, lead a delegation of senior politicians on a mission through Asia. Tokyo would be the first stop. Shortly after receiving this news, we heard from Buchman that a musical play *The Vanishing Island*, would accompany this 'Statesmen's Mission'. The whole party would number between one and two hundred and would be accompanied by all the paraphernalia of a major theatrical production. We welcomed the news, although a little overwhelmed by the prospect of undertaking the largest such project in post-war Japan, especially as the proposed arrival time was mid-June, only six weeks away.

The visit gave an opportunity to involve many people in action and to develop the initiative of many friends. Well-known businessmen like Ishizaka and Ishikawa, the Governors of Tokyo and Osaka, senior political figures and others served on a national committee of invitation; Yamagiwa, head of the Import-Export Bank, headed up the financing for the project; Hasegawa, Foreign Editor of *The Nippon Times*, supervised publicity; and a committee of socially prominent women arranged hospitality in homes – a unique development at that time.

Ichimada took me to call on Prime Minister Hatoyama, who wished to talk over arrangements for a reception he proposed to give for the visitors. Governor Araki of the Bank of Japan planned another reception, and so did the President and Speaker of the two Houses of the Diet.

Since the first large delegation to the Caux conference in 1950, several hundred Japanese had been plunged into the challenging atmosphere of the assemblies at Caux and Mackinac. Now, in the summer of 1955, the spirit of those places was let loose on Japanese soil, and many thousands felt its impact in the theatre, at numerous events and over television. No collection of people like the one which flew into Haneda had ever before invaded Japan. The group comprised not only the cast of the musical, but also an assortment of men prominent in the political life of countries in Europe, Africa and Asia. The cast, too, was made up of well-known actors and actresses and men and women to whom the stage was a novelty. Also in the party were women active in the social life of New York, Boston, Washington and Chicago, and business and professional men from Europe and the United States. About the only thing they had in common was their commitment to live and work for a world remade through a change in people. Many of them were as surprised to find themselves in Japan as were the Japanese to meet them, see them on TV or read about them in the press.

This is how *The Nippon Times* described some of the events of those fast moving ten days of the visit:

' "We come to learn. We come to give." In this spirit, with this purpose, an MRA Statesmen's Mission of 180 persons — representative of 25 countries, speaking 12 languages, from all races — has just completed an historic visit of over a week in Japan. . . .

'Members of the group included John McGovern, for 25 years Labour Member of the British House of Commons, Mahmoud Masmoudi, Minister of State in the Tunisian Cabinet, Ole Björn Kraft, leader of the Danish Conservative Party and former Minister of Foreign Affairs and Chairman of NATO, Dr Oscar Leimgruber, for 14 years Chancellor of Switzerland, B. C. Okwu, Member of Parliament from Eastern Nigeria, and Majid Movaghar, veteran Member of Parliament and newspaperman of Iran, personally representing the Shah on the mission.

'Giving the keynote of the mission on arrival at Haneda Airport, Peter Howard, author of *The Vanishing Island*, said, "MRA is not something the West gives to the East. Nor the East to the West. It is something a man gives to a man. We come to work with you for the fulfilment of Frank Buchman's vision that Japan will be the lighthouse of Asia."

126

'Prime Minister and Mrs Hatoyama received the entire mission on June 15 at their official residence. Eight Cabinet Ministers were present, along with the members of the National Committee of Invitation.

'At the Diet Building on June 15 opposing political parties united in a vivid welcome to the mission. Both conservative parties and both Socialist parties joined in a remarkable reception which extended over a period of four and a half hours, including a visit to the House of Councillors where the mission was officially recognized. The President of the House declared: "In the present situation in Japan top priority and consideration must be given to the reconstruction of our country on the basis of MRA. . . ."

'Thousands of people packed the Tokyo Theatre and later the Kitano Theatre in Osaka to see the new musical play, which dramatizes the convictions of the mission. Members of the Imperial Family attended. The Prime Minister and his wife came, bringing a party of 30 persons. Over one hundred Members of the Diet came. Ambassadors or heads of missions from nearly a score of foreign countries attended. And also a great cross-section of national life in Japan – industry, labour, business, education, youth. . . .

'NHK Television filmed the play and presented it to the nation in a three-quarter-hour programme which included interviews with Ole Björn Kraft, Peter Howard, Takasumi Mitsui, Chairman of the Mitsui Foundation, and Michiko Tanaka, famed Japanese actress, who also plays in *The Vanishing Island*. . . .

'Summarizing the impact of the MRA Mission, a Diet Member commented: "Ten years ago Japan was the target of animosity of the whole world. Now the world comes to Japan and calls her to rise again in the spirit of MRA to help remake the world." '

In an editorial, the newspaper paid tribute to the mission:

'The striking fact about MRA that has been shown by these representatives from all over the world is its tremendous strength, as manifested, rather than in numbers, in the intensive dedication of those who are its participants. Also we are impressed by the character of these people. They are typical leaders in their respective fields – whether it be political, business or anything else – and their outlook is at one and the same time idealistic and practical.

'The ideology of MRA calls for a change – even a revolution – in what we take for granted as human nature. Yet the visit of these leaders from all walks of life and from all over the world has shown there is a great hope for such a fundamental revolution. We have seen and heard enough to prove that the aims of bringing honesty, purity, unselfishness and love into human relations are not far-fetched. We are excited by the possibilities for world peace when these aims are achieved in the relationships of nations.'

As the first plane carrying the VIP's took off from Haneda for Taiwan four Japanese left with them. After some hurried high level negotiations with Foreign Office officials and the embassies of Taiwan and the Philippines, Niro Hoshijima, Kanju Kato, Yukika Sohma and Katsuji Nakajima had secured passports and visas. It was a bold move to include the Japanese. Their reception in Taiwan was uncertain, and in the Philippines Japanese were still feared and hated. Hoshijima, who was now one of the most senior Diet Members, had consulted with Hatoyama before making his decision to go and was encouraged by him to take the risk.

A few days later word came back to us of an historic moment in Manila. At the close of the premier performance of the play Hoshijima stepped forward among the speakers on the stage. At the sight of a Japanese, a shock went through the audience. When it was his turn to speak, a frozen silence descended on the theatre. As he uttered his first words in Japanese, a menacing rumble came from the audience. With Yukika interpreting through her tears, Hoshijima apologized humbly for the past cruelties to the Filipinos. 'Please forgive me,' he said. 'MRA is already building a new Japan, and with MRA all Asia can unite.' The silence ended in cheers. When President Magsaysay received the members of the mission, the Japanese were among them. They also had the opportunity to express their apologies and their conviction of Japan's need for MRA. Magsaysay, a man of great heart and humanity, was moved by their sincerity and two years later, shortly before his death, opened the doors of the country to Japanese travelling in an MRA delegation.

When most of the mission left for Taipei, Kraft and a party of eleven stayed behind with the intention of visiting Korea. There was no treaty of recognition between South Korea and Japan, but there was a liaison office headed by Korean Ambassador Kim. A tall, relaxed and friendly man, Kim tried his best to accomplish an unenviable job. The governments of the two countries were deadlocked over fundamental issues of territory, trade and reparations. No Japanese were permitted to set foot on Korean soil, which had for many years been exploited by Japan. Through Kim, who had seen *The Vanishing Island* and appreciated the work MRA was doing in Japan, Kraft and his party were granted visas at top speed and were assured of a high level welcome in Seoul. The few days they spent there gave them the opportunity to meet a number of senior men and women.

This first arrival of a major MRA contingent in Japan was followed by a second, one year later, when Frank Buchman flew in from Australia in late April, 1956. With him was a characteristically diverse group which included a German prince, Richard of Hesse, a British tennis star, 'Bunny' Austin, an Oxford doctor of philosophy, Morris Martin, a bishop, George West of Rangoon, an actress, Phyllis Konstam Austin, and a young American singing trio, the Colwell Brothers. This was Buchman's eighth visit to Japan, although the last one had been more than thirty years before. He was now in his late seventies, frail, moving around slowly and needing to rest from time to time during the day. But this last visit turned out to be a tribute to his genius for inspiring the leadership of a nation to rise to their best. Many of the nearly six hundred Japanese who had taken part in the assemblies at Caux and Mackinac felt this was their chance to express their appreciation to Buchman. Scores of them flocked around him at the Imperial Hotel, where he stayed, at the events which were scheduled for him and in the brief intervals in between.

When the party flew into Haneda they were greeted by a tumultuous crowd and by some of the country's leadership, including Ichimada, the Katos and Toganos, Hoshijima and other Diet Members. They had come from a Diet in turmoil over the Election Reform Bill, but conservatives and Socialists were united in their enthusiastic greeting of Frank Buchman. The party went straight to a press conference for ninety minutes, which developed into a spontaneous meeting at one end of the airport lobby, with songs by the three Colwell Brothers and short speeches by some of the party, as friends and strangers milled around. At the other end of the lobby another force was in action as red flags and demonstrations speeded a delegation of labour leaders on their way to May Day celebrations in Peking and Moscow.

The next day was supposed to be a light schedule following the long flight from Australia, but it was filled with people. Komatsu, President of the Japan-American Society, telephoned to Buchman to ask him to be his guest at the lunch at which Ishizaka was the speaker. The Colwells were staying in Ishizaka's home and were invited to sing at the lunch. Ishizaka asked to come in for a talk that afternoon. He said to us afterwards that Buchman had congratulated him on the leadership he was giving in the economic life of Japan, but added that he must give equal time to Japan's moral and spiritual development and to the care of his sons. Ishizaka said he would never forget the conversation. He was followed by Sodeyama, President of Toyo Rayon, who told Buchman of the new-found harmony among his management and workers, thanks to MRA. Then came Fujimoto, Editor of the English edition of *Mainichi*, with a group of his reporters for an interview. From that he went straight without dinner into the hotel theatre for a meeting with several hundred Japanese friends which lasted for two hours.

Next morning Araki, Governor of the Bank of Japan, came to pay his respects and the whole party went to be received by the Governor of Tokyo. The Colwells sang and Buchman was given the key to the city by Governor Yasui. From there they went to a 'family luncheon' of sixty given by Finance Minister Ichimada at his official guest house. He had made the generous gesture of including the Katos and Toganos, although the Socialists had just put forward a non-confidence measure against him. That afternoon Sumitomo brought a couple of his senior advisers for tea, followed by Hasegawa, Editor of *The Nippon Times*, for an interview.

Next day, the Emperor's birthday, began with an informal reception for Buchman and his whole party, given by the Prime Minister. That morning Hatoyama showed a side of his nature different from

130

the astute politician. He was a warm-hearted family man and he and his wife had gathered in their home their children and a flock of grandchildren. Frank Buchman was prepared for the occasion. He knew that the Prime Minister was a Christian and a man of principle, but beset by pressing problems at home and abroad, and weakened by physical handicaps. Buchman called on the Colwell Brothers to sing a song in Japanese which they had composed for the Hatoyama family. As he introduced members of his party he had them tell brief, vivid stories of their adventures as they encountered people in different parts of the world. The hour was filled with laughter and some pregnant silences as points of truth slipped home. Later, in an article in the Japanese edition of *The Readers Digest*, Hatoyama wrote of the hour as an 'unforgettable time,' and of Buchman as an 'unforgettable man'.

This was followed by another unusual occasion, a formal luncheon in a Mitsui mansion hosted jointly by the heads of the Mitsui and Sumitomo families. Among the guests were members of both families, as well as the presidents of the Mitsui and Sumitomo companies. Kichizaemon Sumitomo, once so shy that he had difficulty carrying on a conversation, made a courageous speech, referring to his need for change as an individual who had abandoned his responsibilities, and the necessity for management to shoulder moral and spiritual concern for the life of the country. Buchman ended the day by attending the Foreign Minister's diplomatic reception in honour of the Emperor's birthday.

Next day, Buchman was ceremoniously received by Matsuno, Speaker of the Upper House, conducted to the distinguished visitors' gallery and accorded official recognition by the President from his chair, followed by an ovation by the Councillors. Hoshijima told us that was the first time any visitor, other than a state guest or a Parliamentarian, had been given this honour. From the Upper House the party was taken to the Joint Committee Room of the House of Representatives. The visit came at an uproarious moment. The House was in crisis over the controversial Election Reform Bill, which the Socialists were determined to kill. They had just forced two night sessions in addition to the regular day ones and tempers were running high. Fifty Socialist members whose seats were endangered by the Bill had threatened violence and hoped to use the next day's May Day demonstrations to create a riot. The

131

conservatives were considering mobilizing police powers within the Diet, a move reminiscent of the old repressive days.

In this charged atmosphere Frank Buchman created a mood of gaiety and relaxation over luncheon and at a packed meeting afterwards. Hoshijima and Katayama, the two senior members of the major parties, introduced Buchman and referred to the timeliness of his visit. Hoshijima said that MRA was quietly at work behind the scenes to bring a new spirit of what was right. Katayama added, 'To welcome this man of peace at this moment of crisis gives me hope that we will find a solution to the deadlock between our parties.' Buchman gave perspective on this conflict by telling in colourful detail a tale of dramatic reconciliation between extremist opponents in Morocco and Tunisia.

The following evening, at a meeting in the Imperial Theatre, Hoshijima and the Katos and Toganos were able to tell the audience that Buchman's meeting with both sides had been used to prevent violence and produce the beginnings of a common mind between the two parties about how to resolve the crisis. They had spurred the leaders of their two parties to get together to iron out several major points of contention, thus taking the initiative away from the malcontents of both sides.

Buchman went from the Diet to see Princess Chichibu and had an inspiring hour with her, including songs from the Colwells. From her they went to the hotel to find eight of the senior men of Sohyo and Zenro, the two rival national labour organizations. After tea in an upstairs lounge, Takita, Chairman of the 800,000-member Zenro, said, 'This is a different world from the one we have just left, where we were planning turbulent May Day demonstrations.'

The final day, May 1, was a triumphant climax to the visit. It started with Honda, President of the *Mainichi* newspapers, who had planned to look in for fifteen minutes and stayed for an hour, captivated by Buchman's vision for him as a statesman to give the right thinking to Japan. After lunch, with processions of half a million workers parading the streets, Buchman drove to the beautiful azalea gardens of the Bank of Japan guest house for a reception with a dozen of the top financial, business and industrial men. The hosts were Araki and Ishizaka. Shinji Sogo, Governor of the National Railways, had curtailed a trip through the country by six days in order to meet him. Ichimada came, as did Shibusawa, Tadao Watanabe, President of the Sanwa Bank, Governor Yama-giwa of the Export-Import Bank, and Yanagita, President of Japan Air Lines. Governor Araki, introducing Buchman, said, 'MRA has played a most significant role in the post-war rehabilitation of Japan. I pay a sincere tribute to its great achievement in uniting the hearts of nations in the cause of world understanding.' Then Buchman took the men through the years of his friendships with Edison, Ford and Firestone and put it to them that Japan, which had so vigorously used the inventions of these men, should now use the energy and skills of her people to make Moral Re-Armament available to the world.

Buchman hastened from this reception to the Foreign Office where Foreign Minister Mamoru Shigemitsu was waiting to bestow upon him a high decoration, the Second Order of the Rising Sun. As the Minister slipped the ribbon around Buchman's neck, he said, 'It is most gratifying to me to deliver to you the decoration and diploma which His Majesty the Emperor has graciously been pleased to confer upon you in recognition of the meritorious services you have rendered to this country.'

Behind this presentation lay a dramatic confrontation. As soon as Hoshijima had heard the news of Buchman's proposed visit he decided that the Government should recognize Japan's indebtedness to him and Moral Re-Armament by having him receive its highest decoration. He and Ichimada mapped out a campaign. There were three bodies involved in granting this decoration to a foreigner – the Cabinet, Ministry of the Imperial Household and the appropriate embassy. The First Order of the Rising Sun was not often bestowed, but with the Prime Minister, the Foreign Minister and others of the Cabinet convinced of the contribution MRA had made to Japan, Hoshijima and Ichimada saw no problem with the Government acting. But with the American Embassy it was a different matter. We had warned them that John Allison, the Ambassador, was not friendly to MRA. This proved to be an understatement.

When a formal request for a positive recommendation was sent from the Foreign Office to the Embassy the response was negative. Hoshijima and the Katos then called on Ambassador Allison and expressed their strong feelings that Buchman should be honoured. He was at first evasive and then rude and they came away shocked by his prejudice and boorishness. As we pieced the story together later we found that Allison had smeared Buchman and MRA with officials of the Foreign Office and the Imperial Household. He had said that MRA followed the Communist party line, that Buchman was an ambitious self-seeker and was persona non grata at the Embassy. As a result of his violent opposition, the Imperial Household declined to act on the request from the Foreign Office that Buchman be granted an audience with the Emperor and Crown Prince.

The Cabinet was placed in a difficult situation with Hatoyama and other Ministers feeling strongly that Buchman should be decorated, but hesitating to fly in the face of an American ambassador. The Government was careful to maintain the goodwill of her powerful ally and shrank from any open disagreement. The more cautious members of the Cabinet were on the point of stopping any action when Ichimada spoke up. The fiery little Finance Minister lashed out at the timidity which would prevent the Cabinet from following its conscience. Buchman deserved the decoration, he said. They all knew of MRA's value to the country, at home and abroad, and they should not let a prejudiced American official stand in their way. So it was decided to ignore Allison and recommend the Second Degree of the Order, since protocol prevented bestowing the First Degree without ambassadorial recommendation.

The ceremony at the Foreign Office still did not complete Buchman's last day in Japan. There was a final meeting at the Imperial Hotel and then a host of friends went with him to Haneda to see him off at 2 a.m. The impressive outpouring of appreciation from the political, business and labour leaders told one side of the story of this whirlwind tour. Another side was Buchman's unremitting concern for the ordinary man. At a meeting after his departure, the driver of the limousine which had been lent to Buchman said, 'I have been driving for twenty years, but I've never driven for anyone like Dr Buchman. At the end of his last day, as we drove to the airport at midnight, he had me pouring my heart out to him. He gave me a purpose for my life.'

134

12

BUILDING BRIDGES

During the visit Ken Twitchell and I had made to Japan in 1950 we realized that the rebirth of the country – morally, spiritually, socially and in economics – involved her relationships with other countries. The growth of foreign trade, without which her economy would collapse, depended on the reopening of foreign markets; the strengthening of her new democratic institutions required secure foreign relations, otherwise the government was at the mercy of violent subversion at home and intervention from abroad. More fundamentally, the recovery of the spirit of her people called for a purging of the guilt from her wartime actions, recovery of the respect of other countries and her restoration to the community of nations. The 1950 round-the-world delegation had made a small but significant beginning in repairing relations with Europe and the United States.

Restoration of normal ties with most Asian countries was a more serious problem. The 1951 Peace Treaty had declared that Japan must make reparations to the countries she had invaded, leaving the terms to be decided with each of her former enemies. In the early 1950's the payment of substantial reparations was impossible as Japan struggled back from the verge of devastation. But even more basic than this requirement for commercial and diplomatic relations was the healing of the hurts and hates engendered during the war. The Philippines, Malaysia, Indonesia, Burma and, above all, Korea could neither forget nor forgive them.

On the day after my first Christmas with the family in Japan in 1951 I joined MRA colleagues from India, Burma and Thailand for a conference in Rangoon to explore strategies in South East Asia. Prominent citizens had invited Frank Buchman to come with an international team to these countries – a significant gesture at a time when the trend was for Asians to withdraw from close contact with the West.

We talked over the political, economic and ideological situation in the eight Asian countries with which different ones of us were most familiar. We saw two dominant forces at work – Communism, now firmly entrenched on the Asian mainland, and the revolt against the West, which was taking various forms – nationalism, a passion for independence, and a flowering of Oriental religions, especially Buddhism. In this explosive situation we felt that Moral Re-Armament had a great deal to offer. It was a universal idea, bridging East and West; with its emphasis on forgiveness and reconciliation, it appealed to believers of both Oriental and Western religions; it made sense to millions of ordinary people; and it presented to political leaders an alternative to the clash between Communism and anti-Communism. We felt that the invitations to Buchman should be accepted and worked on a report to him recommending that he lead a carefully selected international team through Asia as soon as possible.

A highlight of our visit in Rangoon was a session with Prime Minister U Nu. A devout Buddhist and something of a scholar and philosopher, he had been right-hand man to General Aung San, the patriot who had won independence for Burma from the British at the end of World War II. Aung San and some of his Cabinet had been assassinated by a dissident group and U Nu found himself in charge of a deeply divided country. There were two rival Communist forces, warring tribes and many bandits. He had succeeded in holding the Union together, except for the dissident Karens, but fighting and banditry, when we were in Rangoon, still made it impossible to travel over most of Burma except by plane.

The homes of the Prime Minister and other government officials stood in a compound surrounded by a high wire fence, patrolled night and day by soldiers, since the threat of assassination was never far away. U Nu's round face beamed in a smile as he greeted our host, Bishop West, who introduced us all and told where we had come from. U Nu was immediately alert when Japan was mentioned. He, like his country, had suffered severely in the Japanese invasion of Burma and he had no love for them. He had publicly expressed his opposition to even the most minimal re-armament of Japan. I was able to tell him a few stories of changes

136

in Japanese, especially their repentance for their war crimes –
Kuriyama's and Kitamura's apologies to Congress, honesty and
restitution among government workers and police, and new-found
teamwork in homes and industry. U Nu was interested and
remarked, 'If MRA can grip the leaders of Japan in time with this
spirit, it will modify our attitude towards Japanese remilitarization.'

Frank Buchman responded to the invitations to bring a team to
these Asian countries, and in the summer of 1952 we received a
cable saying he would be arriving in Ceylon to take part in an
Asian Assembly in Colombo in October. He asked us to bring a
delegation of Japanese. This was a formidable challenge, not just
because our friends in the Diet were engrossed in a new session
after the elections; businessmen were struggling out of a recession;
and labour leaders were embarked on another round of wage
demands. Any delegates we took to Colombo must be mature
enough to withstand anti-Japanese feelings and to make friends
out of foes. The party finally was made up of Takeshi Togano and
his wife Satoko, both Diet Members in the Right-wing Socialist
party, Iino, the head of the largest shipping line (persuaded by
Ichimada to join the delegation), Sumi and Hideko Mitsui and
Yasu and Yukika Sohma. Tom Gillespie and I accompanied them.

The conference marked a great advance in establishing MRA as
a significant element in Burma and Ceylon, at the heart of the
Buddhist world, and was officially recognized by the Buddhist
hierarchy. When our delegation entered the ballroom of the Grand
Oriental Hotel we saw a dozen Buddhist monks on the platform
conducting the meeting. The Japanese were ushered onto the platform and Satoko Togano spoke briefly on their behalf.

The day after our arrival the Prime Minister, Dudley Senanayake
gave a reception in the garden of his official residence, the trees
illuminated by hundreds of coloured lights. We were entertained
at a buffet, mingling with many of the country's leaders. The Senate
and the House of Representatives each gave receptions, as did the
newspapers, Port Commissioner, City Council and other officials.
Each morning and afternoon there were assembly meetings and
gatherings for students, businessmen, police and postal and port
workers. The newspapers gave extensive coverage of the events and
the talks at the conference. The Japanese were frequently called on
to speak at meetings and acquitted themselves well, especially the

137

Toganos, who were accomplished spokesmen, and all presented to their fellow Asians a very different picture of their country from the one left by their wartime experiences.

Another delegation of Japanese ventured into South East Asia at the beginning of 1954. Thai leaders arranged a conference in Bangkok, to which Japanese were invited along with delegations from many Asian countries. This time Toyo and Tokiko Sohma led the delegation in which were Senator Yamada from Hiroshima and Suzuki, National Chairman of the Telecommunications Workers Union. The conference was held in the Department of Culture and its Director-General, Luang Vichien, officially welcomed the delegates on behalf of the Thai Government. They came from a dozen Asian countries and among them were some influential men and women – the Speaker of the Malaysian Parliament; from Ceylon a Member of Parliament and the President of the Trade Union Congress; two top Indian labour leaders; and among the Burmese delegation, the Chairman of the Mine Owners Association, head of the government railways and a group of senior Buddhist monks.

From the start the conference took on a public character. The Prime Minister, Pibul Songgram, spoke at one session, and his wife attended a number of meetings and became a close friend of Tokiko Sohma. Among other Thai visitors were the Minister of Education, who was also Mayor of Bangkok, and Prince Naradhip, the Foreign Minister. From beginning to end, the Thai authorites set out to make our stay a model of hospitality, inspired perhaps not only by the natural graciousness of the Thai people, but also because we were meeting at a time of deepening political and ideological tension. The country was surrounded by neighbours in which a shooting war was in progress, and a state of emergency had been declared on her borders with Malaysia, Burma and Laos. The Government seemed to regard Moral Re-Armament as a problem-solving force and wanted to help in every way possible.

Another advance in Japan's relations with her neighbours took place when Hoshijima made his public apology in Manila. Then, as 1955 drew to a close, we found ourselves increasingly involved with Asian countries. During the summer, General Ho Ying-chin and his wife had come to Tokyo from Taiwan. She had cancer and was under the care of a Japanese doctor. They rented a house next door to MRA House and we saw a good deal of them. They felt at home in Japan, where he had studied at the Military College years before, and had many friends in Tokyo. Taiwan was the only one among Japan's former enemies to establish diplomatic relations, signing a peace treaty in 1952 at the insistence of the United States. But there were numerous irritations between the two countries and in the autumn of 1955 the Japanese government decided to strengthen its diplomatic representation in Taipei by appointing Kensuke Horinouchi as Ambassador. We had the Hos and the Horinouchis for dinner. Both couples were committed to seeking God's direction in their lives and in the affairs of their nations. It was an inspiring evening, during which they talked about ways to build a team of people who could work to draw the two countries closer together. Another valuable occasion was a meeting between Ho and the Prime Minister. The General gave Hatoyama a first-hand account of the visit of the MRA Mission to Taipei and the contribution made by Hoshijima and the other Japanese in Taiwan.

In early December another guest from Taiwan came for four days. Milton Hsieh was editor of a Taipei newspaper. On the first evening we gave a dinner party for him with the Hos, the Chinese Ambassador and his wife, the Horinouchis and the Hoshijimas. He met Araki, Governor of the Bank of Japan; Honda, President of *Mainichi*; the Katos and others in business and the Diet. Hsieh talked candidly with the Japanese about the threat posed by the deadlock in relations between Japan and Korea and the Philippines. Communist China and Russia, he said, could thrive on the hates between the non-Communist countries. He suggested to Hoshijima and the Katos that it might be necessary for Japan to take the initiative, especially with Korea, by returning art treasures, relaxing fishing regulations and retracting some of the hard line government statements about Korea. He had especially worthwhile talks with Hoshijima and Kanju Kato, whose respective parties were quarrelling with each other on policies towards Korea.

An opportunity for a gesture towards Korea came at the year's end, when Klaer Widmer, a Swiss girl who was working with us, was invited by a Swiss Red Cross nurse to visit Seoul. She took with her a letter from Kanju and Shidzue Kato in which they made an apology to the Koreans on behalf of the Japanese people for the past wrongs they had committed and pledged themselves to work for friendship between the two countries. The Katos asked that the letter be used with anyone. In Seoul, Klaer presented it to General Choi Yong Duk, Chief of the Air Force, a man of great sincerity and high reputation. The General was moved by its message, 'No ordinary Japanese could have written such a letter,' he said. 'I will see that it reaches the Korean people through the press.'

When Margaret Williams came to visit us in mid-December from Manila, where she was the US Cultural Attaché, she pressed Jean and me to go back with her to the Philippines for a few days to get a first-hand view of the situation and help develop the friendships she had begun making. After Christmas, Jean and I, with my secretary June Lee and a young Australian, Stan Shepherd, flew with her to Manila. Jean and I stayed with Bert and Nanine Oca, head of the longshoremen's union.

The Ocas were generous hosts and we became close friends, talking frankly about their problems at home and at work. He was one of four senior union men with whom Stan and I spent time during our eight days in Manila. They and their wives and several other people became the heart of MRA's team. We had several meals with an older couple, Dr and Mrs Aureo Gutierrez, a doctor and a woman well-known in several fields. Another person of note was Ros Lim, a dynamic young Senator. He was an engaging character, usually in the middle of controversies and political fights, but recently had startled some of his enemies by making a forthright apology to them. We encouraged Lim and Gene Madrigal, the Treasurer of the Trade Union Congress, to fly to Japan to take part in a labour and Socialist conference in Atami, January 8 and 9. Not many Filipinos had yet ventured to Japan.

Atami, Japan's most popular hot springs, nestled on the coast at the foot of the Hakone Mountains. Shoichi Yokokawa, Chairman of the Post Workers Union, who was one of the participants, had arranged for the conference to use his union hostel. It was a potent gathering of sixty union officials, Diet Members and some wives. The meetings were planned and led by Kanju Kato, Setsuo Yamada and Kataoka. Yanagisawa, Yamahana, the Toganos and Shidzue were among those who fought for a new level of commitment at home as well as in political life. Lim and Madrigal made a valuable contribution, giving perspective to the Japanese on their problems.

After the conference the two Filipinos had a busy round of appointments and sightseeing. The highlight of their stay was a dinner given by the two national labour organizations, Sohyo and Zenro, representing the left and right wings of labour, and each antagonistic to the other. Lim and Madrigal spoke from their hearts and did their best to show their freedom from the hurts of wartime occupation by the Japanese. They expressed a desire to see the two countries working together for the welfare of the millions of ordinary men and women they all represented. The visitors also had a down-to-earth conversation with senior officials of the Foreign Office and stated their eagerness to help restore full relations between Tokyo and Manila. On their last day Hoshijima arranged a brief interview with Hatoyama. Lim light-heartedly encouraged the Prime Minister to wage a battle to bring their countries together, and expressed his appreciation for all that Moral Re-Armament was doing to pave the way.

Colleagues in Australia had been in correspondence about the possible visit to Japan of a few prominent Australians who were MRA men. Relations between the two countries were minimal. The majority of Australians were bitter towards Japan, which had come close to invading their country. It was arranged that a Member of the Federal Parliament, Gil Duthie, who was also on the National Executive of the Labour Party, and Lesley Norman, a businessman and former Liberal Party leader in the Victoria State Parliament, would come accompanied by Jim Coulter, a wartime pilot now giving his full time to MRA. Although from opposing political parties, both men had a shared cause for hatred of Japan – Duthie's brother had died in a Japanese prisoner camp in Burma; Norman spent three years as a prisoner-of-war in the notorious Changi camp in Singapore.

On the day after their arrival in March, 1955, Kozo Kimura and Ogata arranged for them to meet Prime Minister Hatoyama. The Australians opened the interview by saying they wished to apologize. Immediately this word was translated the Prime Minister interrupted to say that it was he who should be apologizing to the Australians. They continued that it was not the war years they were referring to but to the period leading up to the war. They felt

141

that at a time when those in Japan who had put their faith in democracy were trying to get the co-operation of the democracies in their desperate economic problems, Australia's policies had been selfish. This they felt had made it easier for those in Japan who were determined to seize the economic initiative by military force to get control.

As a symbol of a new friendship they presented him with a small replica koala bear and told him that they had lost their bitterness and were convinced that MRA offered Japan and Australia an opportunity together to build a new Asia. Hatoyama promptly placed the bear on his large desk and said he would keep it there to remind him of their words. On that same day, the visitors were introduced to Diet Members of the Democratic, Liberal and Right-wing and Left-wing Socialist parties at a luncheon in the Lower House Speaker's Room. Executives of the Right-wing Socialist Party interrupted a meeting to invite them to address them. Norman, after remarking that he and his colleague were members of opposing political parties, said:

'Without MRA it would be impossible for men of such differing policies to find unity. It was in response to an apology by Japanese at the MRA World Assembly at Caux for their wartime activities that we realized our bitterness was equally at fault. We found a new objective above politics in seeking unity between our two countries.' Duthie added: 'What we need is a new element and a new objective right through all strata of our political and national life. It is to live what is right and to change what is wrong through absolute moral standards.'

A few days after the visit to the Prime Minister I had a phone call from Takizo Matsumoto, his American-educated Vice-Minister for Foreign Affairs, to say that Hatoyama wished to give some cherry trees to the people of Australia by the hand of Norman and Duthie. We agreed that this could be accomplished most effectively through a brief ceremony in his Diet office, with TV men and reporters recording the presentation. Matsumoto used the occasion to pay high tribute to the work of Moral Re-Armament in breaking through the barriers of divided countries. Duthie and Norman spoke in warm appreciation of the Prime Minister's gift and said how impressed they had been by the openness of Japan to a moral ideology. The scene was televised at a time when TV was just beginning to become a mass medium.

We gave a reception for the Australians at the MRA House, attended by a group of Diet Members, business and labour leaders and representatives from several embassies. One of the ambassadors turned to me and said, 'You have been here for some time and have had close contact with the Japanese. Tell me, do you think it is possible for them to experience a sense of sin?' I was stunned by his question, but assured him that it was possible, and that I had frequently seen it happen. He evidently regarded the Japanese as a little less than human. No wonder, I thought, that diplomacy often missed its mark.

The visit of Norman and Duthie coincided with the premier performances of *The Boss*. We invited them to speak from the stage at one of the showings and they did so effectively. Norman announced that ex-servicemen and women had contributed towards the purchase of an automobile for the work of MRA in Japan and presented Sumi Mitsui with a cheque. 'Every yen of this one million and a quarter,' he said, 'comes from the hearts of men and women who, a few years ago, were fighting your country. Through MRA they have found an answer to the bitterness they had harboured.'

Then the two met with MRA friends on Easter Sunday before flying home. They spoke of the sense of miracles in the air. Les Norman said, 'I have seen during these two weeks the results of your faith and sacrifice over the past years. There is a team spirit which has been born among you and is flowing out into the nation.' Gil Duthie added, 'Christ is universal, but the way Christianity is lived is often less than that. Frank Buchman broke new ground in the way he presented Christian truths, and here I have seen that clearly demonstrated. I hope we can welcome a team of senior Japanese, trained in this ideology, to Australia.'

When the delegation left Tokyo for the Caux conference in the summer of 1956 it had a new dimension. On the plane were three Koreans – Mrs Hyun Sook Park, the best-known parliamentarian, Dr Park (no relation), dean of a university, and Dr Pyen, a prominent Protestant minister. All three identified themselves with MRA, but it was a traumatic experience for them to mingle with Japanese. All had suffered under the Japanese occupation, especially Mrs

143

Park, whose husband had been caught in resistance work, had been tortured and as a result was a permanent invalid. Dr Buchman had cabled, asking the delegation to fly first to London, where *The Vanishing Island* was being shown at the Prince's Theatre. Most evenings the delegation appeared on stage at the intermission of the play, along with others from many countries. A dozen or more would speak effectively, picturing for the audience a force at work creating unity between nations around the world.

The Japanese were invited to speak at a meeting in the Town Hall of West Ham, in East London. It was packed with an appreciative audience. Some who had lost husbands or sons in the war at the hands of the Japanese came up after the meeting to shake hands with our delegates. At a meeting of the delegation next day Mrs Park got to her feet and in tears told of the pain she had been suffering since she left home because of her hatred of the Japanese. She had been deeply moved by their sincerity and humility and had been overcome by her feelings during their talks the day before. She said she had seen how much she needed a forgiving spirit and wanted to live so that such suffering would never happen again in the world.

The New Year's conference in 1957 at Yugawara in the Hakone mountains, brought together as usual influential colleagues from management, labour and the Diet. Among the highlights of the two days were: a stimulating talk by Takeshi Togano about his strategy for the Socialists in the Diet to press for new ties with Korea and the Philippines, instead of opposing them; candid evidence from husbands and wives of a new spirit being created in their homes; and a maturity among the union leaders, especially in their attitude towards management. An interesting aspect of this gathering was that everyone responded to looking at the national scene from the perspective of Japan's responsibility for her Asian neighbours. Teamwork in home, in industry and in the Diet were important, not only for themselves, but to fit the country to be able to win the respect and friendship of Korea, the Philippines and Taiwan. There was an opportunity to do something immediately about Korea.

Gil Duthie, Australian Member
of Parliament and member of
the Labour Party National
Executive, and Senator Takeshi
Togano of the Right Wing
Socialist Party. Duthie's visit to
Japan in 1955 helped build
important links between the two
countries.

On his arrival in Tokyo, April
1956, Frank Buchman
is welcomed by Hisato
Ichimada, then Minister of
Finance; Setsuo Yamada of the
House of Councillors, and Mrs
Furusawa, daughter of Prime
Minister Hatoyama. Standing
beside Buchman is Takasumi
Mitsui. To the right of Mrs
Furusawa is Shidzue Kato and
the daughter of Mr Ichimada

Frank Buchman (right) greeted by Prime Minister Hatoyama, and Mrs Hatoyama in the Prime Minister's Residence, Tokyo, May 1956. Also L to R. Niro Hoshijima, Speaker of the House of Representatives, and H W (Bunny) Austin

Frank Buchman is decorated with the Second Order of the Rising Sun by the Foreign Minister of Japan, Mamoru Shigemitsu, on behalf of the Emperor, May 1955

The 100-member Japan Youth Federation (Seinendan) delegation with
Frank Buchman at the Mackinac summer conference, 1957

Kichizaemon Sumitomo, senior member of the Sumitomo industrial family, which employed half a million people before the war

Textile workers of the Toyo Rayon Company, Otsu, attend a performance of the Japanese play, "Road to Tomorrow".

13

A PEOPLE'S DIPLOMACY

Later that month, January, 1957, a group of four members of the Korean National Assembly on their way home from the United States were due to arrive in Tokyo, and we had a message that they wanted to visit MRA House during their short stay in the city. They were not prepared to have any personal encounter with Japanese except in the privacy of our home. We welcomed them at Haneda airport shortly after midnight and invited them for dinner the next evening. To dine with them came Hoshijima, Shidzue Kato, the Toganos, Sumitomo, Yasu and Yukika and Tago, head of a steel company. Although they were fluent in Japanese, the Koreans would not use the language and Yukika interpreted their limited English. At the end of the meal our children, Vee and Fred, who were now nine and seven, came in to meet the guests, as they often did, and offered to sing to the Koreans. To our surprise, they launched into a popular Japanese song they had learned, and the effect on the Koreans was electric. They started speaking in Japanese and from a cool and cautious start the evening developed into a memorable occasion.

The Japanese were charming hosts, opening the hearts of their guests with their humility and eagerness to move to a new and creative relationship with Korea. The Koreans responded with forthright convictions about the steps which both countries must take, beginning with Japan. They undertook to work with Mrs Park and Koreans who were identified with Moral Re-Armament. One week later some of them spoke in the National Assembly about MRA's effectiveness in building international friendship.

During the winter we were in contact with our friends in the Philippines who had become interested in holding an Asian assembly in their country. They felt that Baguio, a mountain resort north of Manila, would be the ideal site for it, and wanted to

145

Arnett Branch Library
310 Arnett Blvd.
Rochester, N. Y. 14619

include Japanese in the conference. Early in March a cable arrived from senior Filipinos with an official invitation to Japanese to attend the meeting, March 29 to April 8.

Armed with this invitation, Sumitomo gathered some top level friends for a luncheon. Among them were Ichimada, the Katos, Toganos, Senator Kubo, Hoshijima, Governor Sogo and union leader Yanagisawa. They were enthusiastic – many of them hoping to attend, all feeling that this was the right time for a major move toward closer ties in Asia. Katsuji Nakajima summed up the spirit of the meeting: 'There have been so many conferences at which we Japanese have been on the receiving end. Now is our chance to give.'

It was no simple matter for Japanese to travel to the Philippines. There was no treaty between the two countries and so no regular visas could be given. Fortunately President Magsaysay added his word of support of the conference and his promise that he would attend to give a welcome to the delegates. So the Philippine Liaison Officer in Tokyo was able to arrange for the Japanese to receive special entry permits. Then came a stunning blow – Magsaysay, idol of the Filipinos, was killed in a plane crash. Everything stopped, as the whole country went into mourning. Soon Senator Ros Lim cabled that they were clear that the Baguio meeting should go forward. He had been given a promise by Carlos Garcia, who succeeded as President, that he would visit the conference.

To issue passports for a dozen Japanese to travel to Manila still required a decision at the highest level of Government. There had been a change in the administration. Hatoyama had come under criticism from top business leaders because they feared his liberal attitude towards relations with Communist China and Russia. They also now questioned his ability to give strong leadership because of his poor health. During the previous autumn the largest business organizations demanded his resignation. Hatoyama was able to complete negotiations to restore diplomatic relations with the Soviet, but by the end of the year he could no longer resist the pressures and in failing health resigned. Ogata, who would have been his most likely successor, had recently died and in the internal struggle for leadership Tanzan Ishibashi won and was chosen as Prime Minister, only to retire two months later through illness.

In February, Nobusuke Kishi, supported by business and financial interests, had taken over the premiership. He had come to see *The Vanishing Island* at the invitation of his close friend, the actress and singer Michiko Tanaka, who was a member of the cast. Hoshijima and Tago, the steel men, were confidants of Kishi and had kept him informed about MRA. Now they stressed with him the importance of Japan's participation at Baguio. When Hoshijima consulted him about joining the delegation Kishi warmly encouraged him. At the Diet Members' breakfast the Baguio Assembly was at the top of the agenda and the Toganos, Katos and the rest undertook to speed up the bureaucratic machinery to get all the clearances accomplished in time.

The new Taiwanese ambassador, Shen, and Kim, the Korean representative, were very helpful. The delegations to Baguio from these two countries were of the greatest importance. Kim well knew just how delicate a matter it was for Koreans officially to attend any international gathering at which Japanese were present – it had not happened thus far. He added his word of encouragement with his government to help those in Seoul who were working to get to the assembly.

Against odds, potent groups of Japanese, Koreans and Taiwanese converged on Manila in time for the start of the conference. There were also representatives from most of the Asian countries. Among the Koreans were Mrs Hyun Sook Park, who had been at Caux and was the only woman to have served in the Cabinet; Sun Soon Yoong, Chairman of the Foreign Relations Committee of the National Assembly; and Assemblyman Chun Chung. Former Prime Minister General Ho Ying-chin headed the Taiwanese; the Indonesians were led by the Director of the National Radio, and the Malaysians by the Speaker of the Legislative Council. Representatives from most of the Asian countries bore messages from their heads of state, and the conference took on the dimensions of a semi-official gathering.

Baguio was a popular site for international conferences. Here the South East Asian Treaty Organization had its centre. The mountain air was pleasant after the heat of Manila. (April is the country's hottest month.) The grounds of the Pines Hotel were vivid with tropical blossoms. While the surroundings were serene, the assembly sessions were tempestuous. Although admission to the meetings was by invitation, word soon spread that something unusual was afoot and numbers of Filipinos appeared and sat in the meetings. After a dozen years of silence, here was an opportunity for those who had suffered terror and torture at the hands of the Japanese to unburden their hates and hurts.

Knowing that they would come under heavy fire, the Japanese had mobilized the most mature delegation they could. Among the twenty were Shidzue Kato, Hoshijima, Sumitomo, Kataoka, Yanagisawa and a number of husbands and wives. None of the delegation had been in the Occupation or fighting in the Philippines, but they sat during the first few days quietly listening and accepting the flood of bitter memories, not only from Filipinos, but from the Koreans, Burmese and other former oppressed people. It was a traumatic experience and took all the courage they could muster. Most were in tears much of the time. All that they had to say was: 'We are sorry, we beg you to forgive us, even though you cannot forget. We accept all that you tell us and have determined to live and work in such a way that our country may become worthy of your respect and your friendship.' Jean and I felt for them and marvelled at their grace. Some of the Koreans and Filipinos began to feel the same way. Then they, too, started being honest about the changes they saw were needed in themselves and in their countries if Asia and the world were ever to become secure for their children.

The presence of the Japanese, publicized by the press, had made President Garcia waver, but encouraged by Lim and others he arrived with a large retinue of Cabinet Ministers, Congressional leaders and newspapermen. An international chorus welcomed him and his wife, singing the National Anthem in Tagalog. Garcia sat through a meeting at which representatives of Eastern and Western nations spoke from their own experience of building bridges between races, classes and countries. The President turned to Lim, who was leading the meeting, and said, 'You know, Ros, these people make sense.' He had only planned on being at the assembly for thirty minutes, but stayed for two hours.

The most dramatic result of the conference was what happened between the Koreans and the Japanese. With senior political leaders from both countries present at the express approval of both heads of state, the two groups were able to move from personal reconciliation and the birth of mutual trust to the serious consideration of the major obstacles standing in the way of accord between Japan and Korea. In addition to the legacy of fear and hatred, two especially thorny issues – the Kubota statement and Japanese property claims – stood in the way. The former was a pronouncement contained in a report by a senior Japanese official that the Korean people could be grateful for the benefits they had received under the Japanese occupation. This was assumed by Koreans to be the official attitude of the Japanese government, since it had been published and never contradicted. The property claims amounted to many billions of yen demanded by companies and individuals in payment for their holdings at the end of the Japanese occupation, and the government had supported the legality of these claims for compensation.

Details of a rapprochement between the Koreans and Japanese at Baguio were published in *Yomiuri*, Japan's third largest paper, with a nation-wide circulation:

BEGINNING OF A SOLUTION TO THE JAPANESE-KOREAN PROBLEM
Exploratory Talks between Delegates of both countries at MRA Assembly
(From our Special Correspondent Yamaguchi, Baguio, P.I.)

'Informal talks about the establishment of diplomatic relations between Japan and Korea have been held between leading representatives of the two countries who are attending the MRA Aseembly here, and as a result great hopes have arisen that a way will be opened up to a solution of the various problems between these two countries. The Japanese at the Assembly number twenty, including Mr Niro Hoshijima, Chairman of the Japanese-Korean Society, and Mrs Shidzue Kato, while the five Koreans are headed by Mr Yoong Sun Soon, Chairman of the Foreign Relations Committee and of the National Assembly.

'In view of the fact that these political leaders from Korea were attending the same assembly, Mr Hoshijima had conferred with Prime Minister Kishi before leaving Japan and had come to the Philippines with his consent to use the occasion to launch some exploratory discussions with the view to solving the problems existing between the two nations. Through the good offices of General Ho Ying-chin of Nationalist China, Mr Hoshijima together with Mrs Kato had talks with Mr Yoong and the others for several days, and after hearing the internal situation in Korea and sounding out the views of the Korean government they reached the conclusion that if the Japanese government would first issue a statement retracting the Kubota Declaration and renouncing property claims the way would open to a possible solution, one by one, of the various issues such as the Rhee Line, Takeshima Island and the exchange of detainees.

'In particular, the apology made by Mr Hoshijima and Mrs Kato at the MRA Assembly for the oppression used by the Japanese during the time of their rule in Korea seems to have met with a great response in Korea, and a telegram was reported to have been sent to the Korean delegates by supporters of both government and opposition parties in Korea saying that this action brings hope of the dawning of a new day in the Japanese-Korean talks.

'Mr Yoong stated: "In Korea there are many people who have had bitter experiences of severe torture by the Japanese authorities and are still suffering indescribable illnesses; anti-Japanese feelings run high and there is a strong suspicion of Japan. Through Mr Hoshijima and Mrs Kato we have fortunately been able to learn of Japan's good faith."

'Mr Hoshijima said: "I feel it is impossible to hold unhurried official talks and try to find a mass answer to all the problems; the important thing is to set about solving them patiently one by one. I have been given carte blanche to go to Korea in order to hold preliminary negotiations, and I do not want to miss this golden opportunity of getting closer to each other at any cost. When I return on the 8th I want to talk about future moves with Prime Minister Kishi." '

The significance of this promising start was apparent even before they left Baguio. General Ho, in a talk at the close of the assembly widely published in the press, declared: 'What I and others have striven for in ten years of post-war diplomacy and failed to achieve has been accomplished here in ten days; speaking for democracy, this is the work we are meant to do for many years ahead. The reconciliation between Koreans and Japanese is the most important event of this conference.'

Hoshijima and Shidzue Kato returned to Tokyo a couple of days before the five Koreans arrived en route to Seoul and they decided to get together to talk over the strategy and tactics for advancing what had been started. The Koreans would meet with the Japanese only at MRA House, so on our wedding anniversary, Jean and I gave a lunch for them to which came Kanju and Shidzue Kato and Hoshijima. Our household had prepared a Korean meal, complete with *kimchi*, Korean pickled cabbage – the hottest dish we had ever tasted. The group sat talking a good part of the afternoon. It was fascinating to listen to them going over the issues as red hot as the *kimchi* in a relaxed family atmosphere.

They decided that Yoong, Chung and Mrs Park, who was a personal friend of President Rhee, would give him and the National Assembly a full account of their talks with the Japanese and do all they could to prepare their countrymen to open the doors to negotiations. Hoshijima and Shidzue, for their part, would do the same in their respective parties and Hoshijima would talk with the Prime Minister as soon as he could. Both groups had taken on a tough assignment. The Koreans had to break through an almost universal cynicism about any dealings with Japan; Hoshijima and Shidzue had to try to persuade the government to reverse its stand on the Kubota statement and the property claims. Rejecting the statement meant having to admit that an official government pronouncement was wrong; relinquishing the claims involving bucking a powerful lobby bent on securing maximum reimbursement for its clients.

Hoshijima, like many Japanese, had obtained valuable Korean art treasures in the days when Japan occupied Korea. His most valuable possession was a fine Korean stone lantern. Now, he decided to return it to the land of its origin. His public announcement of this gesture not only evidenced his sincerity about restoring for the past, but started others thinking about doing the same.

During the next two weeks Hoshijima and Shidzue had several conferences. They decided that she, as a member of the Foreign Affairs Committee of the Upper House, would ask questions of Kishi during his appearance before the Committee. Hoshijima would prepare the Prime Minister for the questions and hopefully his answer would provide a gracious means of retreat for the government which would be well publicized at home and in Korea.

What happened is recorded in the official report of the proceedings of the Committee on April 30, 1957:

Chairman, Mr Sasamori: (as the Prime Minister entered) 'Now our Committee will discuss the international situation.'

Mrs Shidzue Kato: 'On this subject I would like to ask you, Mr Prime Minister, a question. We hear that you are planning to visit South East Asia and America in the near future. But before you depart to South East Asia I feel it is very important to solve the delicate negotiations between Japan and Korea, since Korea is our nearest neighbour. At the moment we are faced with deadlock and I would like to know how the Prime Minister intends to solve the problem.

'From March 29 to April 8 at Baguio in the Philippines I had the pleasure of attending a Moral Re-Armament Asian Conference. Many nations were represented at this conference. . . . We had the opportunity to meet many leaders and to undertake, not an official, but a people's diplomacy in the spiritual realm. . . . We noticed especially the delegation of five from Korea. In the atmosphere of the conference we had the opportunity to meet with them on several occasions and open our hearts to each other and I believe we succeeded in initiating a spirit of reconciliation. We were able to establish a feeling of trust between us devoid of any "diplomatic tactics". . . .

'From Korea came Mr Yoong, Chairman of the Foreign Relations Committee (and we believe that his opinions have a great influence on the Political Friends Party) and Mrs Park, former Cabinet Minister, who is a close friend of President Rhee. We had excellent talks with them and through these talks we learned how much the Korean people suffered under Japanese rule for more than thirty years. There is an accumulation of bad feelings, of which we have been largely unconscious. As a result of losing the last war we have learned some of those things, but nothing compared with what they suffered. For instance, Mrs Park's husband who has been a great fighter for the independence of his nation suffered torture which has kept him bedridden for the last eighteen years. These feelings in the Koreans' hearts will not be solved overnight, and there are not a few cases, but many.

'I feel it is important for us to appreciate the feelings of the other person. Of course there are many difficulties over laws and rights of their interpretation, but without first establishing trust we cannot establish diplomatic relations. At Baguio Mr Hoshijima and I apologized for the past. This led to the Koreans opening their hearts and they began to speak Japanese, which they speak fluently, but which they had previously refused to do.

'Mr Hoshijima and I promised them that on our return we would put our best effort, beyond party differences, to tackle the two basic points in the deadlocked negotiations.'

(Mrs Kato then displayed the Government paper *The Korean Times*, edition of April 16, which carried an article positively reporting speeches of Mr Yoong and Mr Chung in the Parliament, following their return from the Baguio Conference, and a United Press news release referring to President Rhee's declaration of the need for a normal relationship between Japan and Korea in view of the common danger of world Communism.)

Mrs Kato (continuing): 'I believe that these responses are the result of the reports of the Koreans who were at the Baguio Conference.

'I hope that in this Committee you, Mr Prime Minister, will declare your sincerity in regard to this Kubota declaration. This statement has given the impression of superiority of the Japanese people to the Korean people. It expresses the attitude of the Japanese as a people, rather than a statement of one person, and as such I believe we should withdraw this declaration.'

Prime Minister, Mr Kishi: 'On this opinion of Mrs Kato over the normalizing of Japan-Korean relations, I agree wholeheartedly on every point with what she has said. When I became Foreign Minister I had many talks with the Korean Minister, Mr Kim. It is my deep regret that we have not been able to solve these difficulties between our countries. Considering our historic and geographical backgrounds it is regrettable that it is so. As far as Japan is concerned, we should try not to hold on to our foregoing assertions but, in the spirit of fairness, we must try to solve the practical issues on the basis of a humble heart. The most important point is not the interpretation of laws, as Committee member Mrs Kato has said, but it is important to create trust on a spiritual understanding, and in this we must take the initiative.

'As far as the Kubota declaration is concerned, it does not represent Government opinion. I have no hesitation in withdrawing it. I regret it has given Korea an impression of our people's feeling superior. I wish to take this opportunity to withdraw that statement officially.'

Mrs Kato: 'I am so grateful to hear that Japan will take positive initiative to clear up our past wrongs, and the next point I would like to mention is about the question of Japanese property claims. Of course, I realize that there are many complications, but Japan, through the San Francisco Peace Treaty, renounced all property except in the four main islands. I realize that this is a big problem, especially for the individuals who invested everything in such property, but this is a domestic problem. I do not doubt that the Government has an adequate plan to satisfy our people, but I would like to hear your opinion about this matter in relation to Korea.'

Mr Kishi: 'As far as this Japanese property claim is concerned, there have been many different legal interpretations of the matter. I wish to state that I have no intention of holding to our past legal interpretations. I would like to face this problem realistically and to solve it on the basis of how we can create future friendly relations between our countries. I do not mean to say that I renounce all juridical interpretations, but I wish to declare that I do not hold to our past point of view.'

Mrs Kato: 'It is quite a task to solve these many outstanding problems, but the most important thing is how we can act with a humble attitude. It is so important to win the trust of the Korean people and I would like you, Mr Prime Minister, to promise that the Government will do its best.'

This gesture by the Prime Minister was reported prominently in the Korean press and was publicly appreciated in their National Assembly. The doors were opened again for negotiations for a peace treaty, long deadlocked. It was to take a few years before all the differences were resolved and a treaty was signed, embracing diplomatic recognition, reparations and commercial agreements. And all through this process the men and women of Moral Re-Armament would continue to play a leading role.

14

ROAD TO TOMORROW

In the mid-1950's the farming population of Japan was declining as many young people moved into the cities, where they could find employment in expanding industries, but agriculture still accounted for more than one-third of the country's work force. It had been a quiescent third. The village families who supplied the backbone of the army until World War II were the post-war stronghold of conservatism, insularity and resistance to change. But the young men and women of rural Japan were themselves experiencing change. Their economic situation was difficult – work hours were long, money in short supply and living conditions relatively primitive. In face of the comparative prosperity of city dwellers the youth of the countryside were becoming restive. Many migrated to the towns. Others began to organize themselves for social action.

Nihon Seinendan, the Japan Youth Federation, was by far the largest and most powerful of such organizations. It had more than four million members, most of them in their twenties and early thirties, including much of the leadership of the villages and towns from Hokkaido to Kyushu. The organization had been resurrected under the American Occupation as officially non-political, its objective the promotion of cultural life in rural Japan. In reality it had become an arena for the conflicts of rightists, moderates and leftists.

Finance Minister Ichimada had been for several years the honorary chairman of the *Nihon Seinendan*, and during one of our visits to his office he urged that we should get to know its leaders. He was concerned about efforts of Communists to take over its leadership. We took his advice, little guessing that the venture would lead not only to a dramatic change in the orientation of Seinendan, but that members of the organization would play a valuable role in further developing a spirit of co-operation in some great manufacturing concerns. Later still, Seinendan colleagues led their powerful membership in helping to resolve a national crisis.

In the spring of 1956, a group from the Seinendan's national executive committee joined the delegation to the Caux conference. From then on, some of them began coming regularly to MRA House to plan how to strengthen the sound elements in their organization. One of them was Zenshu Sagae, a veteran and perhaps its most influential member. He had studied extensively and had a wide perspective on post-war conditions. His mind was continually probing for better ways to deal with the problems his generation was facing. But he was at heart an artist and his chief delight was in working with his potter's wheel.

Soon after we got to know him he had received an invitation from Peking to lead a delegation of farm youth to visit China. Many aspects of the Chinese scene were a revelation to him. He told us of the success of the Chinese revolution in wiping out such social evils as prostitution and city gangsterism. He was impressed by the enthusiasm of the young Chinese and their commitment to improving the life of the country, although he was far too rugged an individualist to accept their regimentation. The most vivid memory of his visit was a meal his delegation had with Chou En-lai. This second most powerful figure in the country had sat with them, unhurriedly talking and answering their questions. Sagae sat with Chou and was astonished when Chou said, 'Mr Sagae, tell me about the pottery you make,' and went on to ask other detailed questions about his life and work. Sagae was amazed, both that the statesman had been so well briefed about him and also that such a busy man would take the time and trouble to concern himself with the young Japanese.

Another regular visitor from the Seinendan was Kinu Wakamiya, a Vice-President and the most powerful woman member. Through her and Sagae, President Sontuku Ninomiya also became our friend. On their arrival from Manila after the Baguio conference, the American trio, the three Colwell Brothers, were invited by him to sing to members of his Central Executive and delegates from the prefectures gathered for a national conference. The Colwells' country music, translated into Japanese, and with new numbers written for Japanese audiences, captured the crowd. They were also given the opportunity to speak, along with Wilhelmsen, Toyo

158

Sohma and others. From then on, almost every day Seinendan members were in and out of MRA House.

One day in the early spring of 1957, Ninomiya came to us to say that Moscow had just issued an invitation to the Seinendan to send five hundred delegates to its international Youth Festival that summer. The Communists on the Seinendan Central Executive had seized on this invitation as an opportunity to indoctrinate a large section of the organization's leadership. Ninomiya wanted to know whether MRA could make a counter proposal. We helped him and his colleagues get off a letter to Frank Buchman proposing that one hundred of the prefectural leaders be invited to Mackinac. This was a venture in faith to which Buchman responded immediately. The young Japanese were in no position to finance their own travel and Buchman did not have the funds, but he knew the calibre of the youth and also recognized the stakes in the ideological struggle for their future. He sent an official invitation and financial guarantee for one hundred to travel to Mackinac for one month's stay and return. Over the next weeks many friends in America, rich and poor, raised the money needed.

This invitation caused a storm at the heart of Seinendan. It was a much more generous offer than the one from the Soviets and was hotly debated in a full scale session of the Central Executive. Nishiyama, the Communist leader in the organization, led a bitter attack, but our friends won the day and the committee voted 85 to 65 to accept Buchman's invitation. This confirmation took place in mid-May, leaving only two weeks for preparations for the delegation's departure to arrive in time for the opening of the Mackinac assembly, a formidable task.

When the dust settled, 104 young men and women had accepted and were cleared for the journey. They represented every prefecture, and most of them were officers of their prefectural committees. Some had responded to the Moscow invitation, but had changed their minds. In the end, only a handful of the Seinendan attended the Communist Youth Festival. For a great majority of them, this was an adventure far beyond their expectations. While they had all demonstrated leadership qualities, their horizons had mostly been limited to their farms, villages, towns and prefectures.

In addition to the Seinendan, some fifty other Japanese set off for Mackinac— Hoshijima, Shidzue, the two Toganos and Senator

Suzuki among them. Governor Sogo of the National Railways arrived there during a business trip to the States. We mobilized every possible interpreter in our team to accompany the youth, since none of them spoke English. Sumi and Hideko, Toyo and Tokiko and Yukika were in charge of the delegation, and also a young man who had recently joined our full time force, Masahide Shibusawa, great-grandson of the Viscount known as the founder of modern industrial Japan and who had been a host to Frank Buchman forty years earlier. Masa had encountered MRA in London when he was working as a representative of a food marketing company, and had come to the conclusion that Moral Re-Armament was the most important work in the world. He expected to meet with resistance from his father, but instead, Keizo invited a group of his friends, including professors and captains of industry, to hear what Masa had to say. At the end of the evening Keizo recalled how his grandfather had left his feudal homestead and plunged into the bracing torrent of the Meiji Revolution. He had seen history being made and wanted to have a part in it. Now, Keizo said, the same blood was running through his son's veins and Keizo supported his decision to throw in his lot with MRA, which he believed was making history today.

Our success in mobilizing the Seinendan was in great part due to Steve, Paul and Ralph Colwell, who were becoming known in wider circles. They had sung on national radio and been interviewed in the press. Now Hoshijima arranged for them to sing for Prime Minister Kishi at a farewell reception before he left on a trip through Asia and on to the United States. Cabinet Members and senior party members from the Diet were present and the brothers made a big hit.

The Seinendan members were the main focus of the Mackinac assembly. The Americans had never seen anything quite like them – and vice versa. Many of the young Japanese felt very insecure, despite the warm welcome and daily care of their escorts. They were surrounded by strange people, strange language and food, and a very different style of life. They were also faced with a challenge to take a look at themselves in the light of absolute moral standards and in the perspective of a world struggle of ideas. Although most of them were politically conservative, some had espoused such anti-American causes in Japan as 'Ban the Bomb', and 'Remove the US military bases'. Some plunged into arguments to blunt the moral challenges with which they were confronted. Some retreated into their own world; they left their watches on Tokyo time – noon in Mackinac was 3 a.m. on their watches – and tried to eat and sleep according to their home time. This was rough on the young Americans and Europeans who were sharing rooms with them and who did their best to communicate, largely by sign language.

At the meetings the Japanese were able to listen through their head sets to the simultaneous translation of the proceedings and at meals there was an interpreter at each table. A number were soon making decisions about their lives, facing such basic problems as stealing, marital infidelity, bribery and hatred, and were experimenting in straightening out what they had done wrong and how to live in the future.

Hoshijima and some of the Seinendan leaders set off for Washington and met with Prime Minister Kishi at Blair House, where he was staying as a guest of President Eisenhower. They told him of Frank Buchman's bold stroke to counter the Kremlin's bid to use the Seinendan and described the impact of the Mackinac assembly on the young Japanese. Kishi regretted that he could not squeeze in a visit to Mackinac on his tight schedule, but proposed talking to Buchman on the phone. Next morning their lengthy phone call was amplified in the Great Hall at Mackinac so that the Seinendan and the rest of the thousand people there could hear the conversation. Kishi asked Buchman what he was doing with the Japanese youth. He replied, 'We are teaching them to go not to the Right, nor to the Left, but straight.' At one point in the conversation, on learning that the Seinendan were hearing his voice, Kishi said to them 'I hope you are fully understanding MRA and will get its spirit in your whole being and take it back to Japan.'

A few evenings later the Japanese electrified the conference by mounting a production of songs, dances and skits. The performance was both a flowering of their personal changes and growing maturity and an interpretation of the best of their distinctive culture. It combined grace, beauty and a good deal of candid humour. Frank Buchman was so delighted with it all that he got to his feet around midnight and said they must give their presentation in the cities they were due to visit, leaving in a couple of

161

days. To any other group the idea would have seemed madness, but somehow, with the aid of round-the-clock work, a stage crew was assembled, a portable stage set was made, halls were booked and invitations rushed out to friends in Detroit, Washington and New York.

A party of nearly 200 – the Japanese, a few Indians and Filipinos and escorts – took off on the night train to Detroit, where they gave part of their show after a dinner by the Chamber of Commerce. In Washington some of the Seinendan had talks with the Deputy Secretaries of Agriculture and Labour and in the evening performed at the Shoreham Hotel for a cross-section of the city. Next day, Senator Wiley gave a luncheon for them in the Capitol and the delegation was received by Speaker Rayburn. The day ended with a dinner and reception at the Japanese Embassy.

After giving performances in New York the party returned via Niagara Falls and Canada to Mackinac. There, one of the older members, Yoshinori Yamamoto, a small town businessman with a farming background, developed the Seinendan skits into a play. It was a simple drama of farm and village life, but realistic and moving because it was based on the experiences shared by many of the group. Its action was set in the home of the Hinomoto family and portrayed the clash between the feudalistic living and thinking of the parents and the post-war attitudes of the children. Disunity in the family was a prelude to division in the village when Hino-moto, played by Seki, the returned Russian prisoner-of-war, refused to listen to other families who asked his help in meeting the water shortage on their farms. During the unfolding of this conflict one of the sons became dramatically honest, with surprising results in the whole community.

One of the young men had the thought that Kay Sumitomo, who had become a friend to many of the Seinendan, should be asked to play the part of a poor farmer who stole water from Hinomoto. Kay was shocked by the invitation. Appearing on a stage was the last thing he had dreamed of doing. He politely refused, but when the cast insisted, he finally agreed. After a shaky start he began to enjoy playing the part of someone at the opposite pole of society from his own. The play, named *Road to Tomorrow*, was not a polished production, but had a compelling reality about it as the cast were portraying a life style they knew well. They performed a number of times at Mackinac before an appreciative audience, and again in Los Angeles on the way home.

When they returned to Japan the play became the focus of their programme. It was not only relevant to the state of the country, but provided a means to mobilize and train hundreds of youth through their national organization. But before the play went on the road several things had to happen. It needed expert direction and production, and again our friend Sugawara stepped in to help. The assembling of a cast who could free themselves from their jobs and responsibilities was a tougher job. To break away from their homes for several weeks, especially after their long absence abroad, was a high challenge. The first step was to return to their homes and act on their convictions to put things right with family, friends and neighbours. Then they might win their support to travel with the play. After two days of conference they left for their families, planning to reassemble in early November.

When they returned they had fascinating stories to tell about their encounters: unhappy relationships had been healed; they had raised new standards for themselves to which others had responded; most had been encouraged to take leave to travel; some had to break through misunderstanding and opposition. All were fortified for the challenging days ahead.

The opening shows were performed in the Daiichi building where *The Boss* had been given, with a preview for some of the leaders of the Seinendan, who were finishing a national conference that day. The visit of one hundred of their members to Mackinac and *Road to Tomorrow* were the most discussed topics at that conference. The Communist opposition to MRA was vocal and bitter. Kinu Wakamiya and President Ninomiya were violently attacked on the ground that they had given the impression they were representing the Seinendan officially at Mackinac. This was merely the cover for the Communists' real concern, which was that they were losing the big gains they had been making in the past two years to take over the organization. But an attempt to pass a resolution censuring Ninomiya and Wakamiya was defeated.

The cast performed valiantly at the première showings and the wide cross-section in the audience responded, both to the play and to the short talks by members of the cast after the final curtain. Invitations came to the cast to perform in Osaka, Kobe and in a number of prefectures, as well as to give shows for such organizations as the National Railways and Hitachi Shipyards. They decided to use the next month for polishing the play and sending small groups to various cities and prefectures to prepare for visits.

The annual New Year's conference was held in 1958 at Kona Hot Springs on the Izu Peninsula, where the Telecommunications Corporation lent their recreational buildings. Among those taking part were our most potent colleagues in the Diet, labour unions and management and a nucleus of Seinendan leaders. There a schedule was developed for *Road to Tomorrow*. The first venture on the road was to be in Ibaraki prefecture, north-east of Tokyo, where Hitachi Electric Manufacturing Company was expecting six performances in three cities where their plants were located. The theatre in the Imperial Hotel was booked for a performance for a VIP audience. The Sumitomos put in a bid for a visit of the play to the Osaka area in early February, aimed especially for the Sumitomo companies. The city of Kobe wanted a visit, and following that, invitations were accepted from several areas in the Southwest, including Hiroshima, the Hitachi Shipbuilding Company, the city of Kure and the Sumitomo copper mining towns on the island of Shikoku. Toyo Rayon was interested in shows for its main plant at Otsu. These were all significant industries, some of them already permeated by MRA, others facing serious labour-management problems.

When the play was launched on the road, the theatres were packed out and audiences spellbound. The cast and the couples who were with them – the Kataokas, Tsurutas and others – were besieged by people who wanted to talk about themselves, their families and their problems after the performances. A great number of individuals and families began to change. Later, cast members received letters from workers, thanking them and saying that for the first time they had found something great to live for. There had been an alarming suicide rate among young factory workers, but one company manager told us some weeks after the visit that since then there had been no more suicides.

Behind the scenes another drama was being acted out. A couple of weeks earlier news had reached the Sumitomo company heads that Kichizaemon Sumitomo was not only performing in the play, but taking the role of a poor and dishonest farmer. The senior men were alarmed, feeling this was a terrible blow to the prestige of the whole Sumitomo empire. Okahashi, the elderly 'supreme adviser', and Tanaka, Kay's personal family adviser, were especially upset. As spokesman for the whole group, Tanaka came to Tokyo to express their dismay and to dissuade Kay from continuing. He met with Kay and Haruko and played on all their emotions of pride and loyalty. Kay told him that it had been his clear conviction to play the part, feeling that it was his responsibility to serve as well as to lead. This was a lesson, he added, which the business world would do well to understand.

The Sumitomo men did not give up their fight and on the eve of the play's visit to Osaka, Okahashi and Tanaka threatened to persuade the companies to withdraw their financial support. Kay's response was not only to stand firm, but to propose that he should speak at the end of the performance to tell why he had played the part. He did so, along with Yanagisawa, who was now National President of the Shipyard Workers Union, and won over the men who had so bitterly opposed him. Tanaka asked if he might have the privilege of introducing *Road to Tomorrow* next evening and in doing so, graciously apologized for having opposed Kay.

From Kobe the party went on to Tamano in Okayama, Hoshijima's home prefecture. They gave four performances for management and workers of the Mitsui Shipbuilding Company and then headed across the Inland Sea to Shikoku Island and the industrial city of Niihama on the north shore. Niihama was the cradle of the Sumitomo empire. There, its first enterprise, the Sumitomo Metal Mining Company, was started. Nomura, chief of engineering, had been at Mackinac with the Seinendan. Again the halls were jammed with workers and their families. They lived bleak lives, many of them in primitive conditions. For two of the performances the cast went up to a village beside the copper mines. The miners and their families sat on the floor. The stage had to be built from scratch. At the end of the show no one made any move to leave, so the chorus and the Colwells sang song after song, interspersed with short talks by members of the cast.

The appearance of Kichizaemon Sumitomo on stage and afterwards, when he spoke, was a sensation to these simple people, almost as though the Emperor had paid them a visit. The management of the half-dozen Sumitomo companies gave a luncheon, a meeting was held with the union heads and then a public meeting chaired by the Mayor of Niihama, at which the impact of the three days in the city was plain to see. On our arrival in town we had found an explosive atmosphere, conflict between the companies and the unions threatening violence. Now the tension was eased and both sides were beginning to explore ways to solve their differences.

Back across the Inland Sea the cast sailed to Hiroshima, where the Mayor and Governor were their hosts. In addition to two performances in the civic auditorium, there were a wreath laying ceremony by the cast at the memorial to the A-bomb victims and a luncheon given by the Mayor and Governor for leading citizens to meet the cast. At the ceremony one of the girls in the cast who had lost her parents and a sister in the atomic blast was among those who spoke. She said, 'This group of foreigners gave me an answer to my bitterness. They showed me that I could have a part in building a new world instead of allowing my feelings to be used by the Communists to create more hatred and tear down society.' The cast went on from Hiroshima to nearby Kure, the naval base, where the authorities said the audience was the largest ever to squeeze into the hall.

Then *Road to Tomorrow* continued its western tour. The cast performed in Ube, near the southern tip of the mainland, for the Hitachi Shipyards and the Onoda Cement plants. They went over from Honshu for a visit to the Shikoku Electric Power Company and other plants, and finally to the main factory of Toyo Rayon at Otsu. During the whole tour they performed for audiences totalling more than 50,000 and wherever they went they stirred hope and brought greater harmony into the homes, plants and communities.

At the showing at Urawa, during the first part of the tour, Governor Shinji Sogo of the National Railways had been in the audience and spoke from the stage very honestly about his dictatorial attitude towards labour, and his desire to change. Also at the show was Koyanagi, National Chairman of the National Railway Workers Union. The two men met after the performance and talked frankly about the problems facing them. The extremists in the union were busy fanning grievances among the workers, aiming at a wave of strikes and slow-downs in the course of labour's spring wage offensive. They agreed that the spirit which had been dramatized on stage that evening was what was needed to bridge the mistrust on both sides. Koyanagi followed up by inviting the cast in the name of the union to perform at the National Railways headquarters for all the key officials of the 450,000-member union when they returned to Tokyo in early March. They invited officers of other unions to be present, and the cast gave one of their best performances. The strikes never happened, and Governor Sogo later credited *Road to Tomorrow* with preventing violence and bloodshed that spring.

While the cast was still on the road the Seinendan had held its crucial elections for its National Executive. Despite bitter campaigning by the extremists, the moderates won a clear-cut victory. Every candidate associated with MRA was elected or re-elected, and from then onwards the strength of the extremists declined.

15

STATESMANSHIP
OF THE HUMBLE HEART

In the autumn of 1957, Prime Minister Kishi decided he should undertake a diplomatic tour through seven countries in South East Asia, as well as to Australia and New Zealand. Consultations between cabinet members and heads of industry had stressed the urgency of developing trade with these countries which was greatly restricted through lack of diplomatic and commercial treaties. Most of these countries had not yet signed peace treaties with Japan, as problems of reparations to them had not yet been settled. Twelve years after the end of the war, Japanese industrial production was already outstripping pre-war records. There was an urgent need to expand overseas markets in order to survive and grow economically. Kishi was hoping his visits would stimulate this commerce.

When the Prime Minister's plans were made public, they brought sharp reactions from two of my friends. On the day before the Tokyo première of *Road to Tomorrow*, Gordon Wise, an Australian colleague who had been travelling through South East Asia, and I had met for lunch with Shidzue Kato and Yukika Sohma. Shidzue wanted to talk over her introduction to the play. When we sat down with the ladies, however, they had Kishi's trip on their minds.

'We feel it is unrealistic,' said Yukika, 'for him to go around Asia talking about trade without first trying to open people's hearts. There's far too much bitterness for them to be willing to enter into business deals.'

'What do you think he should do?' I asked.

'Well, we saw at Baguio,' said Shidzue, 'we wouldn't have got anywhere without humbly apologizing for the past. If Kishi really wants to normalize relations with South East Asia, he'd better begin the same way.'

169

Gordon, who had talked with Filipinos about their feelings towards Japan, agreed strongly with this conviction.

'The only thing is,' I suggested cautiously, 'as Prime Minister, he's going on record officially. Do you think he would really commit himself that far?'

'When I talked with him about Korea,' Shidzue said, 'I think he was sincere in recognizing the need for Japan to make restitution, and he went ahead and withdrew the Kubota statement over the protest of the bureaucrats.'

'But he's sure to run into a barrage from the Foreign Office and MITI (Ministry of International Trade and Industry) if he does anything so unorthodox.'

'That's where we're going to have to help him. Yukika and I have been talking about what we can do.'

Around the table, in that busy restaurant of the old Imperial Hotel, we sat quietly, seeking God's direction on a strategy to initiate a major change in the country's foreign policy – a stroke, moreover, which must be accomplished in the two weeks before Kishi was due to leave. By the time we parted, the ladies had formulated a plan similar to the one which had been successful in breaking the Korean deadlock. Shidzue would enlist Hoshijima, who was now Speaker of the House of Representatives and carried a good deal of weight with the Prime Minister. His part would be to help Kishi recognize that it was vital to put the feelings of people before purely economic considerations. At the same time, Yukika and Shidzue would see Takizo Matsumoto, Parliamentary Vice-Minister for Foreign Affairs, who was helping to plan the trip, and on whom Kishi relied for advice. Matsumoto was an outgoing, open-minded man, and a good friend of ours. It would be his responsibility to do battle with the civil servants who would be deeply shocked at the suggestion of a premier apologizing for anything. Then Shidzue would use her right to question Kishi when he appeared before the Upper House Foreign Relations Committee.

Everything fitted together. The Prime Minister listened sympathetically to Hoshijima; Matsumoto added his word of encouragement and gave him a list of MRA men and women prominent in the affairs of the countries he was to visit, saying that Yukika Sohma had assured him they would be helpful in supporting any initiative which Kishi took; Shidzue was able to open the door for the Prime Minister to indicate publicly his desire to redeem the past. Despite the protests of bureaucrats, Kishi insisted that his prepared speeches be rewritten.

In Manila, the first stop in the Prime Minister's journey, he stunned the Congress by apologizing for Japan's treatment of the Philippines in the war. The day before he arrived in Australia, the press had carried a sharp attack on the government by the war veterans association for inviting a 'war criminal' to the country. On his return, Kishi described for the press the dramatic moment when he stood in the Australian Parliament and began his address with a humble apology, both as a man and as a prime minister, for the harm done by his country to Australia during the war. He said he could feel a change in the atmosphere from cold hostility to a warmth of trust. Overnight the attitude of the Australian press changed from suspicion to cordiality. He experienced the same kind of response in New Zealand and the Asian countries.

In a report to his Cabinet Kishi paid tribute to a 'network of positive and responsive people created by MRA throughout South East Asia.' They had supported him, he said, in his efforts to re-establish confidence. The impact of Kishi's visit was reported around the world. The *Washington Evening Star*, for example, in an editorial on his tour, wrote on December 18:

'Premier Kishi is now back in Tokyo after having completed one of the most unusual missions ever undertaken by a statesman of his rank. Over the past three weeks he has visited no fewer than nine nations that Japan occupied or threatened with conquest ... and in each of these lands he has publicly apologized for his country's actions during the war.'

This was a crucial time in the government negotiations between Japan and Korea, begun some months earlier as a result of Kishi's overtures. There seemed a good possibility that the governments would sign a preliminary declaration spelling out the general issues and the terms on which full treaties could be concluded. On the final day of the year this declaration was signed and paved the way for a slow step-by-step solution of the outstanding differences. Behind this accord lay the goodwill on both sides generated first by

Kishi, Hoshijima and Shidzue, and by the Parliamentary delegation from Korea who were at Baguio.

Our Korean friends had been pressing us to send over a few Westerners to help them in their contacts with their senior friends. We now responded by sending Rowland Harker with two others who were able to stay in the homes of Korean friends. As they were leaving for Seoul, Dr Aureo Gutierrez, accompanied by Stan Shepherd, flew in to Tokyo from Manila. He and his Filipino colleagues had also been at work trying to lay the foundations for an accord between their country and Japan. They had decided that there should be a second Baguio conference to develop the understanding begun the previous year. Gutierrez came to Tokyo to talk over the idea with us and with our friends in Seoul and Taipei. Hoshijima arranged a visit for him with Kishi. Aureo told the Prime Minister of the great value of the Baguio Assembly in drawing Asian nations closer together and said his friends in Manila wanted to improve relations with Japan through a second conference in Baguio in the spring, and hoped Kishi would support sending a strong delegation. Kishi said the earlier conference had had a great effect in creating a new atmosphere between Korea and Japan and he would support a second conference.

After meetings with conservative and socialist Diet Members, Gutierrez set off for Seoul, taking Stan and me with him. We were welcomed with characteristic Korean warmth and grace by friends who had been at Baguio and others whom we had entertained at MRA House. Assemblyman Sun Soon Yoong arranged a number of occasions, the most important of which was an interview with the Speaker of the National Assembly, Li Kee Bong, who was the mouthpiece of President Rhee in the Parliament. We talked candidly about the problems between Korea and Japan. He said he appreciated what Yoong, Chang and Mrs Park had told him about their experiences at Baguio. Aureo urged that Korea be strongly represented at the next Baguio conference.

Back in Japan, Gutierrez continued his pitch for a second Baguio conference with all whom he met and then took off to Hong Kong and Taiwan on the same mission. A few days later he was followed by a fellow countryman, Major Palaypay, Air Force aide to President Carlos Garcia. He had been captured and tortured by the Japanese, but at a Mackinac conference had lost his hatred of them, and now was prepared to do all he could to improve the relations between the two countries. Hoshijima took him to meet the Prime Minister and he reinforced the convictions of Gutierrez about a powerful Japanese delegation to the second Baguio meeting.

As a result of these visits the groundwork was laid for the conference and the dates were fixed for March 18–25, 1958. Aureo had made the bold suggestion that we should include the cast of *Road to Tomorrow* in the Japanese delegation, and our Seinendan friends responded. Hoshijima prevailed upon Morishita, a senior Dietman from the government party to accompany him to Baguio. Morishita was a close friend of Kishi and the Prime Minister sent him as his official representative, giving him a message for the conference delegates:

'In the course of the last twelve months I have had the privilege of visiting many of the countries which will be represented at your conference. I was impressed by the effectiveness of MRA in creating unity between peoples who have been divided. I have myself experienced the power of honest apology in healing the hurts of the past. We need the statesmanship of the humble heart in order to bring sanity and peace in the affairs of men.'

The second Baguio conference was on a larger scale than the first. An impressive number of Filipinos in public life came up from Manila. The Japanese delegation numbered fifty and parties came from most of the Asian countries. Buchman sent a party of Americans and Europeans who were with him in the States, including the casts of three plays. The gathering opened in a more relaxed atmosphere than that of last year – less expressions of bitterness and more positive planning for a united Asia. Many of the delegates held responsible positions in their countries and were concerned not only with personal change, but with relating changes of motive to new policies in their nations.

President Garcia set the keynote in a welcoming message: 'As well as strengthening our economies and defences, we need to encourage an association of Asian peoples which is not directed against other nations but founded on the sure basis of moral ideology.' He sent his Foreign Secretary Felix Serrano to the Assembly. Serrano watched a play and sat through a meeting and responded with an enthusiastic speech in which he said, 'Normally, like begets like, but Moral Re-Armament counters hate and bitterness with devotion and unselfishness. In this spirit we can change the world.'

Morishita seemed overwhelmed with what he encountered. He addressed the conference before leaving, saying, 'Until I came here I had never seen anything so deep, so real and giving new meaning to life in all my fifty years. I had thought that the only revolution was that of Marx and Engels. I ran for the Diet orginally because I wanted to fight for the ending of social evils. I believe that the spirit of this assembly is what we need for the future of our country. I will report faithfully to the Prime Minister all that I have seen here.'

Some of the Filipinos at Baguio were convinced that *Road to Tomorrow* should be shown in Manila. It was a courageous decision, because the public was still strongly anti-Japanese. The Japanese were invited to stay on for several days after the close of the conference to speak at meetings together with other Asians and to mount the play. At such short notice the only available theatre was a large hall in the heart of Intramuros, the old walled city in the middle of Manila, where the Japanese military had put buildings to the flame and slaughtered thousands just before the capture of Manila Bay by the American troops.

The hall was packed and there was a tense atmosphere as curtain time approached. Major Gerry Palaypay stepped onto the stage, as the cast prayed behind the curtain. He told of his torture by the Japanese, his hatred and its cure. He said he recognized in the play and in the spirit of its cast a new Japan with which Filipinos could work to build a new world. The play received an ovation and hundreds poured onto the stage after the final curtain to express their forgiveness and desire to join the Japanese to ensure peace for their children.

Just at this moment, officials of the Japanese and Filipino governments were meeting behind closed doors to attempt to achieve an agreement on reparations, which was essential before the two countries could resume diplomatic and commerical ties. At a dinner at the Japanese mission, given by Ambassador Yugawara, one of the participants in the negotiations, he told the Japanese that discussions had been bogging down until news from the Baguio conference and the response to the play, widely reported in the Manila papers, changed the climate of the meetings and led directly to a break-through in the negotiations.

In less than six months a reparations accord, diplomatic recognition and trade agreements were completed between the two countries. When President Garcia paid a state visit to Tokyo that December to mark the normalization of relations he declared over a Japanese TV network, 'Our ideological and geographical affinities are strong bonds that should hold us together in lasting friendship and enduring peace. It may be truthfully said that the bitterness of former years is being washed away by compassion and forgiveness.'

During the Baguio Assembly the idea was raised of a force travelling in Asia with plays, spokesmen and an international chorus to continue the work of international bridge-building. The delegations responded warmly to the proposal and plans were immediately developed for a mission, going first to Taiwan from Manila in early April, then to Japan, Vietnam, Burma and reaching India by the end of the month.

It was a busy time in Japan to be launching such a mission – campaigning in a general election was about to begin; the annual labour spring offensive was starting up; it was also the eve of crucial elections for the Seinendan's National Executive committee in which again the extreme Left was pitted against the MRA men and women and their moderate allies. Despite all this, our colleagues welcomed the coming of the mission. Hoshijima went at once to Kishi and he gave a message of greeting for them: 'I cordially invite you with your plays, believing that the idea you bring is the most needed one at this crucial time in our history.'

We booked the Imperial Hotel theatre for three nights of plays, as well as lining up receptions, dinners and meetings. The most significant event was a reception given by the Prime Minister. Two days before it took place, Kishi's brother died and Kishi was not able to be at this reception. He asked Takizo Matsumoto to take his place as host. The reception was held in the Prime Minister's official residence and a number of government officials and Diet Members were present. Matsumoto, as Vice-Minister of Foreign Affairs, paid a startling tribute to Moral Re-Armament for its help in regaining for Japan the respect of other nations. He reviewed the successive steps:

1. In the late 1940's the first Japanese to be allowed to travel overseas were welcomed at an MRA conference in the United States.

2. The historic 'Mission to the West' in 1950 re-established contact with Europeans and enabled Diet Members to address the US Congress.

3. The good offices of Frank Buchman and his colleagues provided the only means for Japanese delegates to the San Francisco Peace Treaty in 1951 to meet Asian, American and European delegates.

4. The inclusion of Japanese in the 'Statesmen's Mission' in 1955 was the first opportunity for them to visit Asian countries.

5. The inspired diplomacy of Horinouchi, as Ambassador to Taiwan, had prevented a serious rupture with the Nationalist Chinese government, the one close diplomatic alliance Japan had at that time.

6. The two Baguio conferences gave Japanese the opportunities to establish wide scale contacts with their former Asian enemies and led directly to the diplomatic break-through in negotiations with both the Korean and the Philippines governments.

Summing up this record, Matsumoto said to the group, 'I speak in the name of the Government and of the Foreign Office especially, when I say that at each critical turn we have been aided by the services of MRA.'

Matsumoto drew me aside during the reception and told me that a few days earlier he had decided to run his election to his Diet seat on MRA principles. Then he had gone over the speeches he had been making and eliminated the passages in which he had made bitter references to opposition candidates.

The following month there was another occasion at which Moral Re-Armament's impact on Japan was evaluated, this time by some of the participants, gathered to celebrate the twentieth anniversary of MRA and the eightieth birthday of Frank Buchman. Dr Kajii, Governor of Telecommunications, said that the technical marvels of communication had not been sufficient by themselves to unite the world; it took in addition a great idea such as Moral Re-Armament, which was demonstrating in his corporation its power to unite the hearts of people and create peace.

Governor Sogo told how *Road to Tomorrow* had done much to

Senator Roseller Lim of the Philippines is host at the Baguio Assembly to delegates from Korea, Japan and China, 1957. Left to right: The Hon Sung Soon, Chairman, National Assembly Foreign Relations Committee of Korea; Senator Lim; Niro Hoshijima, Senior Member, Japanese Diet; and General Ho Ying-chin, Chairman of the Military Strategy Advisory Council of Taiwan

Niro Hoshijima with one of the Korean national treasures he returned to
Korea. The return of this ancient stone lion, which belonged to the last
Emperor of Korea, touched on the most inflammatory issues in the deadlocked negotiations between the two countries. Korea's national treasures
were removed to Japan during the Japanese occupation and most of them
found their way into private hands. Hoshijima made the restitution as a
practical step towards the two countries with the expressed hope that fellow
countrymen would follow his initiative.

bring harmony to the National Railways. Miyagawa, head of the Shikoku Power Company, described the healing influence of the play in industrial communities in his part of the country. Yanagisawa, recently overwhelmingly re-elected National Chairman of the Shipyard Workers Union, said that his industry had been permeated by a new spirit between the companies and the union. And Shidzue Kato recalled events of the last few months, saying that we were beginning to see the realization of Frank Buchman's challenge to Japan to become the lighthouse for Asia.

This was the last major event at which Jean and I were present. We had decided that the time was ripe for us to return home. Our Japanese friends were more than capable of taking full responsibility for their programme. Our continued presence might deter them from doing so.

As I listened to the developments our colleagues were celebrating at the meeting, my mind went back over the decade we had spent in the country. I could see that these changes were part of a larger regeneration in the life of Japan. We had stepped into a land still shaken and scarred by war and defeat, occupied by a foreign power and isolated from the world. Now, in 1958, not only were the ruins rebuilt, independence achieved and the isolation ended, but Japan was moving into the front rank of the world's industrial leaders. The quality as well as the quantity of her products was beginning to challenge all competitors. But the changes were more than material and economic. The spirit of the people had been transformed from anxious speculation, unnatural humility and tentative probing to an eager optimism about the future and a confident pride in their present progress.

During the years of recovery there had been some fierce conflicts, disappointments and confusion, but the Japanese people had shown an extraordinary ability to learn from the past and work together to overcome forbidding obstacles. And more than that, the nation had demonstrated to the world a determination to maintain both the freedom of the individual and the discipline of a tightly knit society to make democracy work, despite authoritarian pressures from within and without. They had reconciled in a fascinating way the rival claims of tradition and innnovation, to release an energy soon to command the attention of the world.

In all of this our colleagues had played a distinguished role —

Arnett Branch Library
310 Arnett Blvd.
Rochester, N. Y. 14619

how great a part must be left to be weighed in the perspective of history. For the present we could only be grateful to have become their friends and fellow fighters.

Our last days in Tokyo were typically busy ones, with little time for elaborate farewells. There was a meeting to enlist many in the plans for the summer; the weekly breakfast for Diet Members was marked by new evidence of growing inter-party teamwork. Kanju Kato pledged to Hoshijima, who had been re-elected Speaker of the Lower House, his full support if he continued his fight for what was right. General Ho arrived with the head of the Taiwan Youth Corps to talk over their efforts to take a potent youth delegation to the Mackinac conference. My last appointment was to take Yamamoto, author of *Road to Tomorrow*, to spend an hour with Taizo Ishizaka in his home to tell him about the play's tour and enlist his help in its future moves.

The 'prime minister' of the business world, as he was now often called, was in a reflective mood. He talked of the difficult post-war years, when we had first come to Japan, and when there was so much confusion in the minds of his countrymen about which way Japan should go. Ishizaka said that while he was grateful for the order, reforms and aid which MacArthur brought, he had wondered whether they could survive the speed with which the Occupation was bringing changes. 'Democracy is a wonderful thing,' he said with a grin, 'but the way the Americans brought it to us was rather like filling a goldfish bowl with a high pressure fire hose. The fish became very dizzy and some of them were blown out of the bowl!' He felt that the way we had tried to build on the best of the past, while calling for change, was the most acceptable approach to the Japanese. 'You came at the right time, with the right answer,' he said.

Later, I thought about this timeliness.

Perhaps only those who lived through the post-war years could realize how fragile was Japan's democracy and how close she came to losing the heart of her traditional culture. Without that she would have lost the genius for consensus and group loyalties in face of looming class war and industrial confrontation. It was here that Ishizaka and others of our colleagues helped maintain sanity; they helped make democracy work, especially in the business world. In a giant enterprise like Toshiba the imagination and initiative of an Ishizaka were essential to stimulate and sustain Japan's economic growth. But that growth was also made possible because he learned the prime importance of putting people ahead of productivity, so that his management and the union moved from bitter conflict to demonstrating teamwork to his whole industry. Similarly, in other corporations like Ishikawajima Shipyards, it was the courage and patience of a Yanagisawa that caused the union to challenge management to negotiate on the principle of 'what is right, not who is right,' and so to establish a basis of trust which spread to other shipyards.

Those who may say that the passage of time would have brought integration of the classes within Japan and healing of the enmities with her neighbours, do not understand that there was little time in the turbulent decade of the 'fifties for the leisurely easing of pressures. After encountering the violence of the May Day riots of 1952, the Marxist passions of some leaders of labour, the intransigence of some political extremists of Right and Left, and the pent-up hatred of Japan in the hearts of Koreans and Filipinos, I could never take for granted an amiable course of history. The foundations of democracy were still too frail, the pressures of daily living too acute and the skills of Peking and Moscow too great to allow nature to take its course, undirected by men and women of faith and compassion.

EPILOGUE:

DETERMINED MINORITY

Two years after we left, Japan was faced with a severe crisis, and our friends gave a convincing display of their ability to help pull the country together and lead people on a path of sanity, rather than violence and chaos. In the spring of 1960, the Kishi government was trying to secure the renewal of the Security Treaty with the United States. This treaty had been the greatest single cause of friction between the conservative and Socialist parties ever since it went into effect in 1952. The Liberal Democratic Party, with the support of most business interests, relied upon it as a bedrock of foreign policy and trade. The Socialists regarded it as a sell-out to the United States and the betrayal of a neutralist foreign policy. During 1959 a mounting national debate was waged over its renewal. The Kishi government was strongly in favour of revising the treaty, allowing Japan more authority, while keeping the main provisions. Its opponents formed a well-organized force to stir up public opinion to get it repealed. At the heart of the group were the Socialist Party, the Communist Party, Sohyo, the largest labour union organization, and *Zengakuren*, a militant Left-wing student association. They skilfully pushed themes calculated to appeal to various segments of the populace.

By the time the revised Security Treaty was submitted to the Diet in May the Socialists were entrenched in their total opposition and as the government had a clear majority in the Diet they resorted to parliamentary obstruction and, when that did not work, to physical violence in the Diet. Fanned by the news media and by Leftist publicity, the treaty became the paramount issue around the country. The US Senate had already approved the Treaty and Kishi had invited President Eisenhower for a state visit to Tokyo in mid-June, by which time the Prime Minister had expected the Diet to have ratified the pact. Kishi came to the conclusion that compromise with the opposition was impossible and called a surprise session of the House in the early hours of the morning during a Socialist boycott. His party members at once approved ratification.

Kishi's action caused an explosion of anger, not only in the Diet and among the Socialists, but also around the country. Like Yoshida before him but more flagrantly, Kishi had broken the sacred rules of compromise and consensus. The prime issue seemed not to be the merits of the Security Treaty, which a majority of the voters probably approved, but the manner in which ratification had been handled. The Left-wing forces seized on a perfect opportunity to whip public opinion into a frenzy. With Sohyo in the lead, they orchestrated massive demonstrations and strikes. The *Zengakuren* staged violent protests day after day around the Diet, clashing with the police. In June the treaty came into effect automatically, but public uproar continued, with demands for Kishi's resignation and the cancellation of Eisenhower's visit.

The men and women of Moral Re-Armament who were active in public affairs had become increasingly concerned over the course of events. Although they held differing views on domestic and foreign policies, they were united in their belief that their democratic society was being imperilled and that Japan's relations with her democratic friends abroad were in jeopardy. They decided they must go into action on several fronts.

First, a delegation called on the Prime Minister to voice their convictions and to sound out his intentions and engage his support.

He told them that he had committed himself to stand firm. 'I have decided to risk everything to save the nation from Communism,' he said. While believing in his sincerity, they said that more must be done to put an end to the violence which was threatening Japan's freedom and security. Differences must be settled on the basis of what was right, rather than who was right. Then they went to work.

Shidzue Kato spoke over fifteen stations of the national television network and issued a statement published in *Mainichi*, *Asahi*, *Yomiuri* and other national and regional papers with a combined circulation of more than thirty million. In it she said, 'The Communists, with extremely active backing from Red China and Russia, have tried to destroy the Government by creating a popular front.

Not only that, they have tried to lead the whole country into anti-American rioting so that they could isolate Japan from America.

'The question of whether the Security Pact is right, or whether the action taken by Mr Kishi (in forcing the bill through the Diet) is right, is not the central issue. The real question now is what kind of ideology we want for ourselves and our children. The only such ideology I know is Moral Re-Armament.

'As a Socialist Party member I wish to apologize deeply to the nation for having been too cowardly these past weeks to say what I knew was right. I sat through many meetings and when wrong decisions were made I did not raise my voice. Now I pledge myself to fight all out to save Japan from Communism and create real democracy.'

Senator Kato was a well-known figure, with the largest popular vote in the Upper House, and her stand electrified the country. As soon as her message appeared in print her phone started ringing and thousands of letters and telegrams poured in. Most of them expressed a heart-felt concern for the country and gratitude to her for speaking up so courageously. She was asked to speak several times on television and radio and to contribute numerous magazine articles. *Asahi*, now the largest daily newspaper, reversed its policy in a front page editorial, calling on other politicians to follow the lead given by Shidzue Kato.

Responding to the widespread support she had received, she issued a second statement to the press. It was released to the American press through UPI as follows:

'Everybody in Japan today seems to know what he is against, but what we need to know at the present time is what we are for. From the tremendous response from all sections of the population I realize that a great majority of our people understand and approve my conviction that Japan is not meant to fall into violence and materialistic dictatorship. The only way to create the right authority and strength is through an incorruptible leadership. The strength of Moral Re-Armament is that it makes out of lukewarm partisans of democracy determined fighters for what is right all round the world.'

The June 27 issue of *Life* magazine mentioned assurances by the

Japanese Socialists and labour unions that nothing would be done to harm President Eisenhower, should he visit Japan. It added that the Democratic Socialists agreed to a Kishi truce plan. The magazine said, 'Voices were raised inside Sohyo, the largest of Japan's labour federations, which dominate the Socialist Party, in favour of calling off a demonstration along Eisenhower's route.'

Behind this decisive move was a strenuous effort put up by Renzo Yanagisawa, National Chairman of the Shipyard Workers Union and Chairman of the Association of Independent Labour Unions. He first fought to clarify the basic issues for the 900,000-member independent unions. As a result they passed a resolution welcoming Eisenhower, instead of taking part in the anti-American demonstrations. Then, with leaders of some of these unions, he talked with key men of the Marxist-oriented Sohyo, with its three and a half million members, and they decided to cancel the planned demonstrations.

One further important move was made in the political field. For the first three weeks of the serious rioting the Democratic Socialist Party, which had split from the Socialist Party mainly because of its dissatisfaction with the extremists, remained indecisive in its attitude. Then Shinkichi Ukeda, a Socialist Diet Member, long active in MRA, decided to speak out. At a party meeting he said, 'We must be ruled by the destiny of our nation, not by party politics. Our party must fearlessly stand up and join in welcoming President Eisenhower, and lead the nation to sanity.' Other Diet Members associated with MRA strongly supported him and as a result Chairman Nishio and the party executives publicly agreed to welcome Eisenhower, no longer insisting on Kishi's resignation or the dissolution of the Diet.

A long-time associate of MRA, Susumi Ejiri, Secretary-General of the Japan Newspaper Publishers Association, went into action on the press front. He called together the editors of the major national and local papers at the height of the crisis and told them that they must accept responsibility through their reporting for stirring up the public confusion that made the riots possible. His daily radio and TV newscasts clarified the issues for his large audience. The national press changed its tone at this time, decrying mass demonstrations instead of approving them.

Another phase of the MRA-led offensive was the intervention

by *Nihon Seinendan*. Seinendan was the largest member of the International Council of Youth of Japan, composed of seven million young people from all walks of life. Seinendan leaders who had been at Mackinac and Caux initiated a message from the Council to American Ambassador Douglas MacArthur, nephew of the General: 'The large majority of the nation welcomes the American President with respect and profound appreciation for the assistance America has rendered in the cause of the freedom of Japan. Defying this sentiment, a minor group, manipulated by Communist China and the Soviet Union, and also motivated by political partisanship, is agitating by all means to check the President's visit. It is to be emphatically urged that the ninety million people of Japan, who love peace, will not be represented by such a small group of malcontent politicians and trouble-makers.'

The publicly voiced condemnation of violence and the appeal for moderation by these powerful bodies brought swift results. Violent demonstrations planned in cities across Japan could no longer be held. Some bloodshed continued – one senior politician was assassinated and Kishi was wounded in an attempt on his life – but public reaction swung to opposing lawlessness. Eisenhower bowed to advice not to risk the visit to Japan, but the ties with the United States were maintained. Kishi resigned in the face of his personal unpopularity over his strong-arm tactics. The conservative government stood, with Hayato Ikeda succeeding as Prime Minister. The Security Treaty was maintained. And democratic process survived.

One year later, Kishi visited Caux and paid tribute to MRA's influence on the national scene during the crisis. Addressing the conference he said, 'I was very deeply encouraged that there was a minority of students, labour and political leaders totally committed to the ideology of Moral Re-Armament, who stood straight and fought uncompromisingly for what was right. If there had been an adequate number of such people, such subversive actions could not have taken place.'

And again, one year later, Kishi addressed an MRA conference, this time on Japanese soil. With him were the other three living prime ministers of the post-war years – Katayama, Yoshida, and Ikeda – and some dozen ambassadors, most of them from Asian countries. There, also, was much of the country's leadership in business and labour and a thousand industrial workers. Their presence was testimony to the widespread recognition of a moral and spiritual philosophy which a minority had pioneered during the last dozen years. The struggle of the few to establish their convictions had helped gain for all some firm ground on which Japan was better able to build her great achievements of the years immediately ahead.

INDEX